Predicting Sociocultural Change

Predicting Sociocultural Change

SUSAN ABBOTT AND JOHN VAN WILLIGEN, EDITORS

Southern Anthropological Society Proceedings, No. 13
Gwen Kennedy Neville, Series Editor

The University of Georgia Press
Athens 30602

Southern Anthropological Society

Founded 1966

Copyright © 1980 by the Southern Anthropological
Society
All rights reserved
Set in 10 on 12 point Times Roman type
Printed in the United States of America

Library of Congress Cataloging in Publication Data

Main entry under title:
Predicting sociocultural change.
 (Southern Anthropological Society proceedings; no.
13)
 "First presented as papers in the key symposium
'predicting sociocultural change' at the 13th annual
meeting of the Southern Anthropological Society in
Lexington, Kentucky, in March 1978."
 1. Social change—Congresses. 2. Social prediction
—Congresses. 3. Ethnology—Methodology—
Congresses. I. Abbott, Susan. II. Van Willigen,
John. III. Southern Anthropological Society. IV.
Series: Southern Anthropological Society. Proceedings;
no. 13.
GN2.S9243 no. 13 [GN358] 301.2s [301.24] 79-10193
ISBN 0-8203-0477-8
ISBN 0-8203-0484-0 pbk.

Dedicated to the memory of
John J. Honigmann

Contents

Preface

The contributions in this volume were first presented as papers in the key symposium, "Predicting Sociocultural Change," at the thirteenth annual meeting of the Southern Anthropological Society in Lexington, Kentucky, in March 1978. The task set before the participants was not an easy one—that of dealing creatively with the problem of prediction from various theoretical and methodological perspectives within anthropology. Their responses form an interesting pattern, providing new material for debate and discussion among those anthropologists who support or question the goal of prediction.

The volume is dedicated, as was the annual meeting, to a scholar who would himself have enjoyed entering this discussion. John Honigmann in 1965 wrote letters to colleagues in the South and planned a program of papers as well as an organizational meeting to take place in conjunction with the 1966 annual meeting of the Southern Sociological Society. In so doing he founded the Southern Anthropological Society. As the society grew, John Honigmann continued to provide leadership, encouragement, hard work, and wise advice until his death in 1977. It was with deep appreciation and sincere gratitude that the society voted to dedicate the 1978 meeting and proceedings to this outstanding man and eminent anthropologist, who set an example for us all in his life of dedicated service to the profession and to the quest for knowledge.

Gwen Kennedy Neville
SAS Proceedings Editor

Predicting Sociocultural Change

Introduction:
Predicting Cultural and Social Change

SUSAN ABBOTT

This volume represents an experiment. The experiment involves predicting directions of social and cultural change. The purpose guiding these attempts is to illuminate and test the robustness of a variety of theories and methods brought to bear on the task of prediction. A primary goal is to stimulate thought regarding prediction of change in sociocultural systems.

The ability to predict the behavior of systems, whether physical, biological, or social, is seen by many as the mark of a mature science. An extensive literature in the philosophy of science addresses the problem of prediction (e.g., Hempel 1965; for a contrasting view see Scriven 1962). The view that prediction is a desirable goal has its champions within anthropology. Anthropologists advocating prediction typically are adherents of a tradition whose roots lie in Anglo-American empiricism, which emphasizes the use of descriptive and quantitative methods applied to groups or individuals in specific situations. Scholars in this tradition typically make predictions which they hope to verify. Examples of work representing this view are multiple (see Honigmann 1976: 392–94 for an overview of this orientation, including citations of particular scholars following in this tradition). However, I consider work by those interested in decision models of social structure to be better than most when the specific problem is prediction (e.g., Fjellman 1969; Geoghegan 1969, 1970).

In contrast to the empirical approach, others say the proper business of anthropologists is "thick description" and the interpretation of particular cultural traditions in ways that will make them sensible to those not reared in those traditions (e.g., Geertz 1973). The decoding of meaning systems and subsequent translation into alternate meaning systems, in fact, remains a primary if not singular activity of an important segment of the contemporary anthropological community. In their ranks are adherents of structuralist, symbolist, and some cognitive traditions. If culture is conceptualized as concerned only with the cognitive order, then questions become irrelevant that regard culture as a set of emerging systems built on the observation of frequencies of patterned behavior and on processes of development and change (Tyler 1969: 13). Tyler states that "So construed, neither prediction of actual events nor specification of developmental process is a necessary component of a theory of culture (1969: 13–14)."

When anthropologists move into the area of endeavor labeled applied anthropology or, alternately, "policy-relevant" research, the ability to predict becomes central. This ability is central because those agencies and institutions requesting the help of applied anthropologists expect us to be able to predict. We must therefore seriously, thoughtfully ask ourselves, "Can we successfully predict non-trivial directions in sociocultural change?"

As organizers of the symposium out of which this volume grew, John van Willigen and I believe that the topic is timely because many anthropologists are openly acknowledging a desire to be directly or indirectly involved in the application of anthropological knowledge to current and future social concerns. We need to think critically, therefore, about the limits to our ability to predict both long- and short-term changes in social and cultural phenomena. One might logically begin by examining the ability of a variety of theories and methodologies to aid in prediction.

One would presume that among the theories and methods currently available, some are superior to others for the task of prediction. The contributors to this volume were selected because they use divergent theories and methods. The charge to each of them was quite specific. Drawing on his or her own field data, each was asked to attempt to predict directions of change in any part of a social, cultural, economic, or political system of personal interest. All were charged to be theoretically and methodologically explicit, since the goal of the volume is to present for evaluation the limits and strengths of these theories and methods.

In order to stimulate critical thought, two discussants have presented formal comments. As a means of highlighting the interdisciplinary nature of the problem of prediction, we chose discussants who are not formally anthropologists, though both are sympathetic to the concerns of anthropology. One has recently authored a book on the problems of prediction in the social sciences (Henshel 1976). The other, Strodtbeck, has extensive cross-cultural research experience and control of the anthropological literature. Because they discuss each contributor's relative success at accomplishing the task set for all, I will not do so in this introduction.

The first two chapters concern themselves with social roles, but they approach the topic from quite different perspectives. Harding and Clement are interested in the cognitive structuring of roles, while Gallaher is concerned with changes in role content through three generations. Harding and Clement feel that prediction of the specific content of roles is overly fraught with difficulty and therefore is not profitable, while Gallaher attempts that specific task.

Nardi calls attention to a potentially powerful technique for predicting directions of change in her paper on computer simulation. She offers a thoughtful critique of some current, widely publicized simulations produced by economists and political scientists, drawing attention to the potential dangers in too ready a reliance on these formal methods.

The authors of the next two chapters make use of aspects of cybernetics and systems theory. Daniels tries to predict the fate of pastoral values among Kenyan Kipsigis, and Gerlach is interested in predicting the predominant form of social organization and change in American postindustrial society. Both are concerned with the effects of industrialization on local communities with relatively little power to control energy.

In the next paper Pessar attempts to approach the problem of predicting the future of millenarianism in Brazil, using three kinds of symbolist analysis. According to Pessar, the fate of millenarianism depends on the definitions placed on it by those in political power at the national level. She concludes that standard symbolist theories are too imprecise to allow prediction; they are far better suited to the purposes of logico-meaningful analysis.

In the final contribution, in an attempt to predict the future of the inhabitants of one small part of the Navajo reservation, Adams tries out several theories favored by culture historians and general ethnologists. Adams's final assessment seems to move him into the arena Pessar occupies. The root of the problem is that the important political, economic, and social forces affecting Navajo life on the reservation are beyond Navajo control (as they are beyond the control of Pessar's millenarians, Daniels's Kipsigis, Gerlach's North Dakotans, and Harding and Clement's Ixil). What the American government will decide to do with the Navajo depends on Americans' current conceptions of themselves. Americans' history of fear, domination, and subsequent incorporation of admired, presumed attributes of the Indian into their self-conception forms the basis of this peculiar fate for the Indian. This is also the cause of Adams's inability to predict. He states that Americans as a people do not know what or whom they want to be. In order to adequately predict what will become of the Navajo and all American Indians, one would have to come to understand the relationship among the symbolic system in process, the political economy, American national character, and national history.

As Henshel points out, these efforts are all pioneering ones. Some are more successful than others when it comes to prediction, but they are all stimulating reading. Most of the authors commented that they did not find the task we set them an easy one. Most also remarked that it made them think about their data in new, stimulating ways. It is van Willigen's and my sincere hope that this collection will have a similar effect on its readers. In conclusion, I echo Strodtbeck's remarks that the combined efforts of these scholars make evident that good applied work—that of the sort requested by those who wish to utilize our understanding of social and cultural process—rests on the foundations of strong basic anthropology. There are no possible short cuts.

REFERENCES

Fjellman, Stephen J., 1969. Talking about Talking about Residence: An Akamba Case. Paper presented at the University Social Sciences Council Conference, University of East Africa, University College, Nairobi.

Geertz, Clifford, 1973. *The Interpretation of Cultures* (New York: Basic Books).

Geoghegan, William, 1969. Decision-Making and Residence on Tagtabon Island. (Working Paper No. 17. Language Behavior Research Laboratory, University of California Berkeley).

————, 1970. Residential Decision Making among the Eastern Samal. Paper presented to the Symposium on Mathematical Anthropology, 69th Annual Meeting of the American Anthropological Association, San Diego.

Hempel, Carl, 1965. *Aspects of Scientific Explanation and Other Essays in the Philosophy of Science* (New York: Free Press).

Henshel, Richard L., 1976. *On the Future of Social Prediction* (Indianapolis: Bobbs-Merrill).

Honigmann, John J., 1976. *The Development of Anthropological Ideas* (Homewood, Ill.: Dorsey Press).

Scriven, Michael, 1962. Explanations, Predictions and Laws. In *Minnesota Studies in Philosophy of Science,* vol. 3, H. Feigl and G. Maxwell, eds. (Minneapolis: University of Minnesota Press), pp. 170–230.

Tyler, Stephen, ed., 1969. *Cognitive Anthropology* (New York: Holt, Rinehart and Winston).

Regularities in the Continuity and Change of Role Structures: The Ixil Maya

JOE R. HARDING AND DOROTHY C. CLEMENT

Cultural adaptation occurs in response to pressures affecting the stability of a sociocultural system. The nature of this response, in turn, structures the potential for subsequent change so that change is permitted yet continuity is maintained. We are concerned here with predicting patterns of continuity and change in role structures, particularly with predicting patterns of cultural adaptation as reflected in the cognitive role structure of the Ixil Maya. We are concerned both with predicting specific changes that are likely to occur and with predicting the manner in which change will occur in general. We focus on the accumulation of low-level adjustments and choices among alternatives which allow for gradual change in the system of cultural belief while higher-level cultural rules remain relatively stable over time. From a systems perspective, we argue that general-level rules, which allow for alternative ways of conceptualizing problems and opportunities and thus for system flexibility, are more stable than specific activities subsumed by them. We predict the specific ways certain new roles would be received were they to be introduced into the Ixil area and what the probable future course of two existing roles will be. Analysis focuses upon both inter- and intraethnic group variation and upon findings and predictions from a study conducted by Harding (1973). That study was designed so that its findings and predictions could be tested by replication.

Several data sources have contributed to the development of the present analysis. Archival research giving important time depth has been published by Colby and van den Berghe (1969) on interethnic relations in the Ixil area. The earlier work of Lincoln (1945) provided valuable data about the recent past. The particular data upon which this paper is based are the result of ethnographic field work conducted by the authors in 1968 and 1969. Clement studied divination, curing practices, and settlement of conflict during the summer of 1968. Harding worked in the Ixil area for a year, from the fall of 1968 until the fall of 1969. His general ethnographic work focused on culture change, Ixil and Ladino (non-

Indian) role structures, and *cofradia* (religious brotherhood) activities. Toward the end of this year, a focused ethnosemantic study of roles and activities was conducted. Data on role terms and activity concepts and their interrelationships were obtained from both Ixil and Ladino samples and included a total of some 750 informants. The techniques used in the ethnosemantic portion of the study evolved from the methodological approaches of cognitive anthropology for elicitation and analysis of semantic domains and more general aspects of systems of belief.[1] A detailed description of the methodology for eliciting data and of techniques for a portion of the analysis employed in the Ixil study is provided in Harding (1973; see also Harding 1974). The present paper makes use of a combination of data from both the ethnographic and the ethnosemantic investigations.

THE ENDURANCE OF THE IXIL

The Ixil, a Maya-speaking population of the west central highlands of Guatemala, live in the *municipios* of Nebaj, Cotzal, and Chajul in the department of El Quiché. Within this area they constitute approximately 92 percent of the population, and the remaining 8 percent are primarily Ladinos.

The study of Ixil culture is particularly interesting and rewarding because ethnohistorical data are available for a period of more than 450 years, and limited archaeological investigation in the region has extended our knowledge still farther into the past. Ruins in Nebaj, including tombs and earthen pyramids, have yielded evidence of a socially stratified population inhabiting the area during a period which reached its zenith in the tenth and eleventh centuries (Smith and Kidder 1951). Ethnohistorical records reveal that the three present-day Ixil towns of Nebaj, Chajul, and Cotzal were all well established in 1530, when they were conquered by the Spanish. (See Lincoln 1945: 45–46, and Colby and van den Berghe 1969: 41.) This information and that derived from archaeological sources may indicate that the Ixil were politically and socially organized, perhaps along theocratic lines similar to other Mayan groups (Lincoln 1945: 56–57).

As with the rest of Latin America, the Ixil area underwent drastic alterations resulting from the Spanish conquest. Depopulation was particularly severe, a fact that aided the Spanish colonial officials and *encomenderos* (large landholders, the Spanish equivalent of lord of a fief) who worked in tandem with missionary orders to consolidate control. Municipal structure was reorganized; indigenous parishes were established; the traditional religious practices, particularly those involving sacrifice, were disrupted; *cofradias* were established; and the missionaries attempted to substitute the Catholic calendar for the Mayan and replace Mayan statues and ceremonies with Catholic saints and rituals.

Pre-Conquest patterns were not totally dismembered, however. Spanish power waned in the mid-seventeenth century and the Ixil were left relatively isolated for the next 250 years. As a result of this semiindependence from Spanish control, and later from national Guatemalan control, the Ixil were able to maintain certain pre-Conquest institutions and cultural practices that were lost in other areas. The syncretism of Catholicism and native Ixil practices constituting the religious structure still in practice today became entrenched during the early part of this period. The Ixil also retained use of the Mayan 280-day calendar, which is still used for scheduling of religious ceremonies and for divining. Emphasis on ancestor worship has been maintained and the *cofradias* became, from the orthodox Catholic point of view, mere festive and recreational centers for men (Lincoln 1945: 129). According to Lincoln's informants, elements of a pre-Conquest caste system (composed of warriors, priests, workers, and possibly merchants) also survived until the turn of the present century with top *principales* (high-status persons) being descendants of the warrior families. During the late 1890s, chief *principales* collected tribute from lower-caste individuals, primarily in the form of labor (Lincoln 1945: 58–61).

Ixil culture, with its clear continuity with the archaeological past, provided a distinctive system with which the Ixil faced the next onslaught from the non-Maya world. This came in the last years of the nineteenth century and continues to the present.

PRESSURES FOR CHANGE

We are now witnessing the alteration of Ixil culture, brought about in large part by the entry into the Ixil area of descendants of the Spanish who so altered the area 450 years ago. The relative isolation and autonomy of the Ixil from national economic and political development ended rather abruptly as coffee gained ascendancy as a cash crop in Guatemala. Laborers were then needed to work on coffee *fincas*. Supported in their ventures by the reestablishment of compulsory labor laws and debt peonage, labor contractors pursued this opportunity for economic gain primarily among the Indian populations of Guatemala (Colby and van den

Berghe 1969: 72). Beginning in 1894, Ladino labor recruiters came to the Ixil region.

Gradually, ties to the outside increased and the Ixil area became more vulnerable to governmental programs and policies. The end of Ixil isolation also has meant the influx of foreign goods and ideas including radios, evangelical missionaries, foreign militant priests who began a concentrated effort to reconvert the Indians through an indoctrination program, schools that teach the Ixil that Columbus discovered America, a clinic, an all-weather road (completed in 1946) which links the area with main Guatemalan highways, mail service, telegraph service, and regular bus service. More basic pressures for change, however, are seen in the patterns of Ixil-Ladino interdependency that have developed since the influx of the Ladinos. This interdependence is primarily in terms of economic and political organization. Economically, Ladinos control extensive land holdings and some of the key supply and distribution channels, including almost all trucking, for the majority of commercial goods moving into and out of the Ixil area. Ladinos are wholesalers to Ixil storeowners and are also the primary money lenders, charging interest of up to 15 percent per month.

A few Ixil have been able to use this new system to their own advantage. There are a few wealthy Ixil landowners and a small number of Ixil involved in trade activity related to Ladino enterprises. Ixil who are merchants, artisans, craftsmen, or large landowners constitute a small percentage of the population, however. By and large, most Ixil practice subsistence farming supplemented by employment as day laborers on local farms, contract laborers to the coast, domestic servants to wealthy individuals, or helpers to artisans and craftsmen.

For the majority of Ixil the acquisition of land by Ladinos over the past ninety years, coupled with a high rate of population increase and soil depletion, has resulted in a marked reduction of the amount of land available per person. Because of the limited amount of land, these Ixil are no longer self-sufficient. Corn farmers, with their traditional methods of slash-and-burn agriculture, find their patterns less viable than in the past and are unable to provide sufficiently for themselves and their families without participation in Ladino-controlled economic institutions.

Patterns of social relationships also reflect Ixil interdependence with the Ladinos. The wealth obtained in this new system is in part redistributed to poorer Ixil through patterned dependency relationships. Persons of wealth in Nebaj, most of whom are Ladino, are looked to by the Ixil as sources of employment and credit. They are requested to serve as godparents of Ixil children (the *compadrazgo* relationship) and they become involved in enduring patron-client relationships. There is also a certain amount of interethnic concubinage. Ladino institutions (e.g., wage labor) and instrumental relationships with Ladinos where the Indians take the subordinate role (e.g., the patron-client relationship), offer alternatives to the traditional Ixil institutions and social relationships. At the same time the establishment of the Ladinos in the Ixil region has reduced the viability of traditional patterns. For many Ixil, participation in these alternative forms appears to be the only option.

In comparison with economic patterns, Ixil patterns of combining religious and political control have better survived the intrusion of Ladino institutions. Lincoln (1945: 71) states that the Ixil priests held control of the municipal government until the early part of this century. Gradually, Ladinos assumed an expanded role in local government, and by 1924 ethnic dualism was fully incorporated and the priests had lost control of the municipal government. The Ladinos now control the highest position, the *alcalde* (mayor), but this has been accommodated by the Ixil recognition of the highest-ranking Ixil as the *alcalde natural*. The Ixil attribute equal status and control to this position, which by Ladino standards is clearly a secondary one. This and other status-conferral systems are independent of the Ladino evaluative framework. For example, the selection of *mayordomos* (heads of the religious brotherhoods) continues to be made by the Ixil high priest (*b'oq'ol b'aalvastiix*) in combination with the Ixil *principales*. The head *b'aalvastiix* also plays a role in the Ixil religious ceremonies that are connected with the municipal government but not sanctioned by the government. The *cofradia* system, along with the practice of *costumbre* (traditional religious ceremonies) is still quite strong. *Costumbre* is conducted by *"Catolico"* (traditional) families for the house, for planting, for their ancestors, for a death, or for protection against possible adverse events that signs indicate might befall a person or a household. Ixil priests have a role in these aspects of religious life as well as in marriage and in the settlement of conflict through divination. Curing rites are also conducted by the *b'aalvastiix*.

Despite its strength, the ceremonial-civic leadership complex of the Ixil is not without its competitors. The evangelical religions and the *catequista* or "new" Catholic movement, which was introduced and pursued by foreign priests, both attempt to attract the *Catolicos* away from traditional practices and reconvert them. The hospital clinic and Western doctors and pharmacies also constitute an alternative to the curing aspects of the *b'aalvastiix* role. Some *b'aalvastiix* see their work in curing and the work of the Western doctor as being in conflict.

Several trends have been presented in this section. In short, we see that the system imposed by Ladinos has resulted in the decreased viability of the traditional means of life practiced by the Ixil. The problems of economic survival force the Ixil into interaction with Ladinos and the Ladino-controlled institutions that link them to the outer world. Ixil control over their own religious and political structure has been weakened, though not destroyed, by the Ladinos and faces competition from religious and medical institutions brought in from the outside. In the face of these pressures, we are prompted to ask what may be expected with regard to continuity and change in Ixil culture. What aspects of the Ixil's knowledge, belief, and system of values are being maintained? What sorts of alterations is it undergoing? In the following, we narrow the focus to asking, What are the patterns of change in the cognitive role structure?

PREDICTING PATTERNS OF CULTURE CHANGE

In the analysis of continuity and change in Ixil role structure, we are aided by a variety of developments in the systemic view of culture and society and in the conceptualization of roles. A key conceptualization has been the clarification of roles as objects of ongoing negotiation rather than as static, well defined scripts for behavior. Our position is consistent with that presented in Buckley (1968), which includes an integration of the theoretical formulations of Gross, Mason, and McEachern (1958); Secord and Backman (1961); Turner (1962); Strauss et al. (1963); and others.

In this conceptualization, roles are seen as tools of interaction which constantly undergo negotiation as to which specific activities or actions can be incorporated or engaged in the name of the role. As Herbert Blumer states it:

> the Human being is not swept along as a neutral and indifferent unit by the operation of a system. As an organism capable of self-interaction he forges his actions out of a process of definition involving *choice, appraisal, and decision*. . . . Cultural norms, status positions and role relationships are only *frameworks* inside of which that process [of formative transaction] goes on. (1953: 199–201, as quoted in Buckley 1968: 498–99)

Because the social constructs of roles are general, they allow for this negotiation and thus the fitting of different alternative elements into structural positions at various times.

Other work may also be cited which reveals the more basic, but more general, nature of roles. The research of Francesca Cancian (1975) demonstrated in Chiapas, for example, the flexibility that people have in altering the activities that are associated with social identities. She defines an identity as "a 'role' that covers a relatively broad range of actions and that includes assumptions about the probable motives or reasons that explain the actions of that kind of person" (1975: 137). In the social identity approach she takes, there is an assumption that people conform to the normative behavior associated with roles "in order to obtain validation for particular identities from certain others" (1975: 146). Her data support the propositions that "an individual's beliefs define an important identity, and are shared with others who validate the identity" (1975: 149) but that commitment to an identity and conformity to its associated norms does not necessarily involve internalization of the norms. In other words, *"norms* (or collective definitions of [the activities associated with] an identity) *can change rapidly and without intensive interaction"* (1975: 141, italics hers).

The idea that role activities are negotiated places roles at a higher level of generality than is the case when they are thought of as being stable, static, well-defined entities. It means that although there is a general concept of the role, the activities engaged in by an individual to whom the role is attributed are affected by the individual's interpretation of the environment at a particular time. As Buckley points out (1968: 504), this organization of roles allows for the kind of flexibility necessary for social systems to adapt.

This reconceptualization of the notion of role meshes well with what is now known about how people conceptualize roles. In addition to research indicating the flexibility in alteration of role-associated activities, we also know something about the nature of the more general conceptualization of roles relative to one another or, in other words, the cognitive structuring of these roles. As has been found from similarity data for certain other domains, (D'Andrade et al. 1972; Clement 1974), role terms are organized not by referential meaning, but rather by associated, pragmatic characteristics. When people are asked to judge the similarity of roles, the criteria they use are broad underlying dimensions which correspond to socially important dimensions of meaning in the society. Burton's work (1972; Burton and Romney 1975), for example, suggests that for American English speakers the dimensions of evaluation, power-solidarity, and occupational status seem to be important in similarity judgments of role terms. Harding's (1973) data from Nebaj shows that the Ixil and Ladinos also give evidence of similar underlying dimensions by which role terms are organized.[2] For the Ixil the dimensions, as might be anticipated from the ethnographic work, appear to be wealth, ceremonial-civic stature, and externality (alien, versus local, person). Salient dimensions for the Ladinos appear to be morality (moral-immoral), involvement of physical labor (physical labor versus nonphysical labor), and, as with the Ixil, externality. The dimensions are continuous and intersecting. Thus, *b'aalvastiix* (Ixil priest, prayer-sayer, diviner), for example, is seen by the Ixil as similar to other roles which are local, ceremonial-civic, and poor. In the Ladino role structure the salient aspects of *b'aalvastiix* in terms of the dimensions are local, physical laborer, and mid-position on the morality dimension.

These dimensions of role structure correspond to broad patterns of interaction and expectation. Goodenough (1965) argued for the Trukese, for example, that roles were grouped into clusters which were owed various patterns of deference and respect. Similarly, we find for both the Ixil and Ladinos that general patterns of expectation and treatment associated with roles correspond to various positions in the cognitive role structure. For the Ixil, for instance, the wealthy are viewed as potential *compadres* (child's godparents), employers, sources of loans, and recipients of deference in social interaction. Those having ceremonial-civic roles are accorded respect, regarded as knowledgeable, and expected to intercede between the people and supernatural or extraneous forces.

The cognitive data, as can be seen, complement the arguments recently made by those analyzing the nature of roles. The underlying dimensions of the cognitive role structure do not determine which activities will be associated with which roles; they exclude certain possibilities, but do not specify which of a number of alternative combinations of activities would be appropriate at a particular time. A general framework is present within which individuals negotiate among possible alternatives.

The pattern in cognitive role structures is also interesting in the correspondence it bears to the organization of belief systems as suggested by Rappaport (1971a, b; 1974) and Bateson (1972). The generality of cognitive role structures relative to the activities associated with roles is analogous to Rappaport's suggestion that cultural rules and concepts vary in their specificity. General beliefs serve as legitimators or organizing formats for lower level rules. Because they are vague, these general beliefs allow for alternative lower level rules and thus flexibility in the system. Bateson suggests this phenomenon as well—that the more general structure is stable and guides the incorporation of new ideas, thus allowing for continuity while flexibility is maintained because of the vagueness of the basic-structure conceptualizations. Applying their conceptualizations to cognitive role structures, then, it is quite feasible to argue that we can expect greater stability at the more general conceptual level and that greater value will be attached to the more general level. In other words, people will be more accepting of lower-level changes in behavior. It is thus possible to change in response to social, economic, or political pressures, yet maintain continuity with the past.

This argument has obvious implications for predicting general and specific change in role structures. Namely, it is to be expected that the cognitive role structure will be more stable than will be the structure of activities associated with the roles. Roles will tend to cluster more similarly over time even though the activities associated with them may, and probably will, change. This is a general prediction that can be made about patterns of change in cognitive role structure.

Partial support, in fact, is available for the stability argument from the Harding (1973) data collected on the distributional similarity of roles. In correlating perceived role-role similarity and perceived activity-activity similarity, greater agreement was found for roles than for activities. This was true for both the Ixil and Ladino samples. To conduct this test for the difference in agreement on role and activity distributional similarity, the sample consisting of 166 Ixil and Ladino respondents who completed the "roles by activities" beliefs matrix was divided into 16 age-sex ethnicity subgroups (i.e., Ixil-Ladino; then male-female; then ages 15–25, 26–35, 36–45, and 46+).[3] The individual matrices within each subgroup were aggregated, and the distributional similarity of each role pair and each activity pair calculated. Then, the intercorrelations between each set of subgroups were calculated for the resultant aggregate role similarity and activity similarity matrices.

The intraethnic, intrasex intercorrelations for role and activity distributional similarity are presented in table 1. Support for the hypothesis is indicated in that only 2 comparisons out of 24 are in the reverse direction from that predicted.

The disagreement or intracultural variability found in the activities data cannot be unequivocally equated with instability in activities, given the possible alternative interpretation that the disagreement is due to different positions of the subgroups in the life cycle. It might be possible, for example, that younger people have only limited knowledge of what activities are associated with a given role. It is reasonable, however, to rule out this alternative, since the variability should be associated with role-role similarity as well. The indications from both the Ladino and the Ixil data, in other words, support our proposition that cognitive role structure is more stable over time than the activities associated with the roles.

In addition to predicting the general pattern of role structure stability, it is also possible to make certain predictions regarding the future of individual roles—both those which are currently recognized as represented in the area and those which are conceivable but as yet nonexistent in the area. Once we have ascertained the basic dimensions important in the role structure, it is then possible to use these dimensions as a basis for assessing the future of a given role.

Table 1. A Comparison of Rank-Order Intercorrelations with Ethnic and Sex Sub-Samples for Role and Activity Distributional Similarity (R×A Matrix)*

Age	IXIL (N=92)		LADINO (N=74)	
	Roles	Activities	Roles	Activities
	Men (N=47)		Men (N=37)	
15-25:26-35	.864	.752	.779	.731
15-25:36-45	.887	.791	.763	.664
15-25:46+	.888	.794	.690 <	.735
26-35:36-45	.930	.879	.837	.809
26-35:46+	.917	.909	.727	.652
36-45:46+	.923	.890	.746	.724
	Women (N=45)		Women (N=37)	
15-25:26-35	.875	.865	.808	.766
15-25:36-45	.840	.703	.818	.785
15-25:46+	.874	.797	.810	.796
26-35:36-45	.862	.799	.861	.760
26-35:46+	.826 <	.889	.809	.691
36-45:46+	.858	.806	.878	.877

* No significance test was computed for the difference between correlations. Note, however, that the differences are large in most cases and probably significant since the number of cells being correlated was 1225, i.e., $\binom{50}{2}$, for the roles matrices (number of roles=50) and 1128 for the activities matrices (number of activities=48).

We know from general ethnographic research and from cognitive elicitation data that roles are associated by the Ixil with dimensions of (a) wealth, (b) ceremonial-civic stature, and (c) externality or association of the role with aliens versus local persons. Since general expectations and treatment owed to people vary according to these dimensions, the shift of a role in this structure over time would probably coincide with an alteration of the treatment accorded persons holding that role. Analogously, we propose that reaction to the introduction of a new role can be ascertained by examining the qualities of the role (and roles seen as similar to it) in terms of the dimensions important in the culture where the role will be introduced. Thus, for both nonexistent and currently existing roles, we argue that it is possible to anticipate future positioning of the roles based on knowledge of the cognitive role structure and anticipation of structural changes in the society. Since we know which aspects of a role are important to the Ixil, for example, we can project Ixil reaction to the role in the future.

The following section constitutes an analysis of and projections for three roles, two of which existed and one of which was nonexistent at the time of the 1969 study.

THREE ROLES: PROJECTIONS FOR THE FUTURE

Two existing roles in the Ixil area which might be considered crucial or pivotal indicators of change in Ixil culture are the roles *b'aalvastiix* and *catequista*. At least in terms of continuity with the past and the maintenance of unique aspects of Ixil culture relative to that of the intrusive Ladino culture, the future of these two roles is extremely important.

B'aalvastiix. The role of *b'aalvastiix* encompasses a set of activities, not all of which any one *b'aalvastiix* performs. The general role includes *b'oq'ol b'aalvastiix* (Ixil high priest who keeps the Maya day count and determines ceremony dates), *b'aalvastiix* (ceremonial prayer-sayer, sometimes curer), and *'aq'i* (calendar priest and diviner). The *b'oq'ol b'aalvastiix* has substantial knowledge of the Maya calendar and traditional religion. Some of the *'aq'i* use the Maya calendar in their work with divining problems and diagnosing cures for people's problems. They serve as important enforcers and reminders of traditional conceptualizations of interpersonal conflicts and violations of religious strictures. The *b'aalvastiix* has a part in some civic and neighborhood rituals as well as in individual and family ceremonies relating to such things as planting, ancestor worship (and spirit appeasement), marriage, and death; or as an intermediary in certain situations such as asking for a loan. For the Ixil, the *b'aalvastiix* is an integral part of certain aspects of daily life and performs important activities which are part of community events and community organization.

In terms of underlying dimensions, the *b'aalvastiix* is seen by the Ixil as being a highly ceremonial-civic role, unlike roles such as evangelical missionary and buyer of archaeological artifacts (*comprador de camaquiles*). As with *mayor-domo,* the prestige and respect associated with *b'aalvastiix* as a ceremonial-civic role contrasts with another underlying dimension, that of wealth. Though wealth is positively valued, *b'aalvastiix,* along with other Ixil roles such as *comadrona* (midwife), *juntador de copal* (incense gatherer), and *cushero* (maker/seller of illegal liquor), are placed on the poor end of the wealth dimension. The lack of wealth of the *b'aalvastiix,* in contrast with other roles such as *finquero* (large landowner), *extranjero* (foreigner), and even to some extent *alcalde natural* (Ixil "mayor"), corresponds to information obtained in ethnographic work suggesting that *b'aalvastiix* tend not to be wealthy. Although Lincoln suggests that Ixil priests had extensive civic control during the early part of the century, there is no indication of gains from such control being associated with present-day priests. Instead, it appears that, if anything, Ixil priests have lost any access they might have had to control of governmental jobs and therefore to past opportunities to benefit from right of corvée (labor) and knowledge of indebtedness and land availability.

Ladino attitudes toward the *b'aalvastiix* reflect their lack of knowledge of or appreciation for the priest's knowledge and position in Ixil culture. They tend to equate the role with a *brujo* (witch) and consider the *b'aalvastiix* to be equivalent to other low-status Ixil.

Several predictions can be made from these data. We can predict that the position of *b'aalvastiix* is fairly secure. It is unlikely that the *b'aalvastiix* will become wealthier, that they will cease to be thought of as having ceremonial-civic aspects, or that they will become identified with outsiders. We would not expect the positioning to change unless the *catequista* movement garners many additional supporters. On the other hand, the role as we know it today may change in the sense that the kind of knowledge controlled by the *b'aalvastiix* may change. Possibly because of such things as absence of lure of the role in terms of wealth, the transmission of traditional knowledge in the form of apprenticeships (which are quite time consuming) appears to be diminishing. The *b'oq'ol b'aalvastiix,* for example, had in 1969 just lost an apprentice because he could not manage to learn all the prayers while at the same time consuming the amount of liquor required as part of the ceremonies. At that time, the *b'oq'ol b'aalvastiix* was worried about the lack of prospects for other apprentices. Fewer *b'aalvastiix* who do divination and curing may now know the calendar as well as earlier practitioners, and instead may use other methods of divination. We would also expect the content of curing and perhaps divination to change because of competition from alternative sources of curing made available through the pharmacy and clinic. (See Landy 1974 for analysis of this type of content adaptation of roles.)

In summary, the Ixil are dependent on the *b'aalvastiix* in a number of areas of their lives, yet the rewards of serving as a *b'aalvastiix* do not promote the acquisition of wealth, which is an important assessment criterion for roles. Mechanisms for assuring rewards and for encouraging mastery and maintenance of the traditional knowledge are weak, perhaps as a result of the changes brought about by the Ladinos. Thus, we can predict that under *present* structural conditions, the role of *b'aalvastiix* is unlikely to undergo a redefinition relative to other roles, yet its content will gradually change, particularly in the erosion and replacement of traditional religious knowledge now incorporated into the *b'aalvastiix* activities.

Catequista. Catequistas, as previously described, are militant "new" Catholics who have been reconverted by Catholic priests in an attempt to attract them away from traditional practices. For the Ixil, they stand in contraposition to the *b'aalvastiix* as one of the more attractive alternatives to traditional Ixil culture, primarily because the role offers positively valued aspects of Ladino life while at the same time maintaining certain characteristics which are important and valued in the Ixil way of life.

Catequistas are both Ixil and Ladino. Many Ixil who became *catequistas* are encouraged to do so by the Catholic priest who aids them in elementary school and in some cases helps them to secure more advanced schooling which necessitates going outside the area. The *catequistas* thus have a reputation for literacy. Through ceremonial activity and other contact with Ladinos, some Ixil catequists became *cambiados de ropa* (those who dress and act like Ladinos) although they are not considered as low status as are noncatequists whose main role designation is *cambiado de ropa*. Ixil catequists are encouraged by Ladino catequists in entrepreneurial activities and are thought of (according to the judged similarity[4] verbatims elicited in the 1969 study) as having more economic success in working with Ladinos than do the average Ixil. Another factor, which may make a difference in possible prosperity of the catequists, is that they are forbidden to participate in traditional ceremonies. Whereas traditional Ixil are spending increasing amounts of money on traditional ceremonies, the catequists, though they spend some for the ceremonies and processions which Acción Católica stages, are able to use a much larger portion of their earnings for personal advancement. This, combined with their learning of alternative economic/entrepreneurial skills, may allow them to increase both their wealth and their status in nontraditional activities.

The positioning of *catequista* in the cognitive structure reveals some reasons why this role is seen as being generally positive even though some Ixil see catequists as causing conflict and quarrels with traditional Ixil. The Ixil see *"catequista"* as positioning almost identically with "Ladino" on the dimensions of wealth and externality. Both are viewed as wealthier than *naturales* (Ixil) and as neutral on the dimension of externality. On the other hand, the role has an important quality; it is seen as being ceremonial-civic in nature, thus deserving of some status. It is interesting to note in this regard that the catequists stage processions, as do the *cofradias*. The evangelicals do not stage such processions and are not perceived as holding a ceremonial-civic role.

The role of *catequista* is viewed positively by the Ladinos as well. For the Ladinos, a *catequista* is seen as being almost identical with a *cambiado de ropa* in that both are considered nearer to the local than to the alien end of the externality dimension. The Ladinos, however, see the *catequista* as much more moral than the *cambiado de ropa*. In fact, they see the *catequista* as being a moral role relative to most other roles. For the Ladinos, the status of the *catequista* is comparable to that of a principal, one of the higher-status Ixil roles from the Ladino point of view.

The future stability of the *catequista* role in the cognitive structure, and its future in providing an attractive alternative to traditional Ixil roles, depends in part on the success or lack of success of the economic pursuits of those who join the catequist movement. As argued above, it is likely that the *catequistas* will fare better than other Ixil in acquiring positions that pay more and in gaining the support of Ladinos in these ventures. Since they are kept out of the cargo system of the traditional Ixil, they are spared the leveling influences of holding a *cofradia* office. On the other hand, one wonders how many sources of income yet remain in the area that are not already being exploited. The *catequista* is also left without the defenses of the traditional Ixil in the event of sickness or other untoward occurrences. Dependence upon these measures, including the *b'aalvastiix*, in times of stress is not likely to be foregone. Thus, a failure of the promise of the *catequista* alternative to materialize could cause the group to vanish and return to traditional ways. On the basis of present evidence, however, we can project that the *catequista* role is a strong competitor for Ixil allegiance. Although its proponents oppose it to traditional Ixil patterns, we see that the role actually incorporates characteristics that are highly valued among the Ixil. Both wealth (relative to non-*catequista* Ixil) and ceremonial-civic stature are associated with the role. Thus, the role allows greater access to economic positions controlled by Ladinos and entails abandonment of certain traditional practices yet, paradoxically, draws its appeal from its congruence with underlying Ixil values.

Demostrador de Productos Agricolas. The nonexistent role chosen for study was selected to represent an alternative to the life of the average Ixil, yet not one which necessarily entails rejection of the religious pattern of life or requires that other patterns of Ixil life be shunned. At the same time, the role offers the possibility of greater economic prosperity for the individual Ixil involved and possibly for other Ixil as well. The role, *demostrador de productos agricolas* (person who demonstrates agricultural products [and techniques]), was suggested as a possible new role by Ixil informants during initial elicitation work concerning the domains of roles and activities.

In this section we will attempt to predict how this role would fare should someone attempt to introduce it into the Ixil area. Again, as in the sections on existing roles, the projections are based both on assessing the manner in which the role fits into the cognitive role structure and on the conditions of social structure that would affect the feasibility of such a role. The information used in developing predictions thus comes from general ethnographic data and from the cognitive elicitation work.

It is possible to collect cognitive data on nonexisting roles because of the potential of language for describing things which have not been experienced. Thus, it is possible to insert descriptions of new items into a list of existing items about which associational data are being collected so that reaction to the new items can be compared with reaction to the old.[5]

"Demostrador de productos agricolas" translates, roughly, as "agricultural demonstrator." An analogous role in this country might be the agricultural extension agent. As with other nonexistent roles tested in the original research, the role was viewed differently by the Ixil and the Ladinos. This is evident from a comparison of roles seen as similar for the Ixil versus the Ladino which are presented in table 2. There is little interethnic group agreement on roles seen as similar to a *demostrador,* nor is there much overlap in highly associated activities. However, with this role, in contrast with some of the others tested, there is not a large difference in its general valuation. In general, it is ranked upper-middle range in preference[6] by the Ixil, and lower-middle range by the Ladinos. The major difference is that Ixil and Ladinos apparently have different ideas of what the role would entail and of what kind of person would hold it.

The Ladinos, it is projected, would expect the role to entail a combination of businessman, teacher, and occupationally skilled person. Because the role is seen as similar to roles which are "alien," the Ladinos might anticipate an outsider in the role. The Ixil, on the other hand, envision the role as being somewhat ceremonial-civic, an insider, and a person who is reasonably wealthy for an Ixil. The person is seen as being helpful and knowledgeable. The commercial aspect attributed by the Ladinos is missing for the Ixil.

These assumptions that would be made about a *demostrador de productos agricolas,* we assume, would inform the behavior of an Ixil or a Ladino toward a person holding such a role. Marked discrepancies be-

Table 2. Roles similar to *Demostrador de Productos Agricolas*
(from Roles by Activities Matrix)*

FROM IXIL MATRIX ONLY

Similarity

Value	Item
.917	Tocayo
.917	Catolico
.909	Alcalde Natural
.906	Principal
.904	Maestro
.901	Ayudador de Gente
.897	Albañil
.888	Amigo

FROM LADINO MATRIX ONLY

Similarity

Value	Item
.911	Contratista
.908	Dueño de Tienda
.900	Maestro de Pinturas
.897	Maestro de Musica
.886	Finquero
.883	Viajero
.880	Comprador de Camaquiles
.880	Comerciante

FROM BOTH IXIL AND LADINO MATRICES

Ixil Value		Ladino Value
.917	Carpintero	.869
.905	El que Ofrece Ayuda	.869

* The ten most similar roles were taken from the Ixil aggregate R×A
matrix (N=92) and the Ladino aggregate matrix (N=74).

tween the expectations and the actual characteristics of the role would
undoubtedly bring about a reconceptualization. Our predictions that the
Ixil, for example, would expect a *demostrador* to be somewhat wealthy,
a local person, and a person of some ceremonial-civic stature, and would
thus treat the person as they treat others who have similar combinations
of traits, are predictions of preliminary behavior only. Should initial con-
tacts show the role holder not to meet these expectations, a reconceptualization would occur.

SUMMARY AND CONCLUSIONS

In considering how cultural systems respond to changes in the environment, we are forced to ask how continuity and flexibility for change are simultaneously maintained. A framework suggested by Rappaport (1971a, b; 1974) and Bateson (1972) meets these criteria. Different levels of specificity of belief are posited so that the more inclusive levels are general and abstract and therefore are able to subsume a number of alternatives at the less inclusive levels. In addition, these higher, more abstract levels are described as being valued. They command more commitment and for that reason, as well as because of their generality, are relatively stable. The lower-level beliefs, on the other hand, are seen as more specific and more easily foregone in the face of changes in the environment.

This conceptualization of cultural systems, when applied to the study of role structure, meshes quite well with recent efforts to reformulate the concept of role and the ongoing dynamic processes of which roles are a product. In the same manner, cognitive data on role conceptualization provides an understanding of the organization of roles at a general rather than a specific level. This research indicates that role similarity is conceptualized according to basic underlying dimensions of meaning which correspond to expectations for general treatment and action.

These data and conceptual formulations have led us to suggest that cognitive role structures will be more stable over time than will be the associations between particular activities and particular roles. This suggestion is supported in part by data from the Ixil area which, as described in the early part of this paper, has undergone massive change in the last seventy to ninety years. New roles and activities have been incorporated into the cognitive role structure, and old roles altered in terms of the activities associated with them. At the same time, a large degree of continuity has been maintained and, we predict, will continue to be maintained owing to the relative stability of the overall role structure. We can also depend upon this structure to predict the general response of people to a new role or to old roles which have been affected by structural or social changes in the system.

It should be noted that our argument implies that specific response to roles can best be predicted from specific information on the activities to be associated with a role.[7] According to our argument, the more general structure cannot tell us exactly which of the many possible alternatives will be selected at a lower level. Furthermore, since these aspects of culture may change fairly rapidly, our predictions of the associations which will be made between roles and activities decrease in certainty as time passes. Prediction of general patterns on a long-term basis is more assured. We can expect that in the face of even massive change, the underlying role structure will persist, channeling the potential for incorporation and recruitment of new roles; yet we cannot predict exactly what activities, what exact content, will come to be associated with those roles.

The dimensions underlying the cognitive role structure of the Ixil Maya, particularly the ceremonial-civic and wealth dimensions, are conceivably of great antiquity. It is possible to see how these dimensions can persist in the face of massive change in the social and political environment and in an extremely intrusive contact situation. It is also possible to see how the dimensions can persist while the particular content—including the aspects of Ixil culture, such as the use of the calendar, which are of interest in illuminating the pre-Columbian past—can be replaced by other content derived from outside sources. Thus, for example, the *catequista* movement provides a source of opportunity which demands that the Ixil shun traditional practices, yet it manages to incorporate elements of roles which Ixil value, thereby meshing with traditional dimensions of Ixil culture.

NOTES

1. See Sturtevant (1964), Colby (1966), Black (1974), and Durbin (1974) for overviews of these approaches and related research. The particular combination of techniques and analysis utilized in this portion of the study grew out of work by Stefflre (1972; see also Stefflre and McClaran 1967, Stefflre, Reich, and McClaran-Stefflre 1971) which was elaborated in this and other studies (e.g., see Harding, Clement, and Lammers 1972, 1973; Clement et al. 1973; Clement 1974; Harding and Boyer 1976).

2. Determination of the underlying dimensions of the cognitive role structures was accomplished in the following manner. Roles and activities were elicited heuristically (see, for example, Stefflre, Reich, and McClaran-Stefflre 1971; Metzger 1973; and Harding 1974 for detail on these procedures) using question frames of the type: "What types of people are there?" and "What types of things does X [type of person] do?" Subsets of the role-domain and activity-domain items were then selected as components for a "roles by activities" ($R \times A$) beliefs matrix. Respondents were asked to relate these items to one another by a standard question frame calling for a yes or no response (i.e., "'Y' [activity] is done by 'X' [role]; yes or no?"). By combining every role with every activity for the 50 by 48 $R \times A$ matrix, a respondent answered 2400 questions concerning his or her perceptions of what activities are appropriate for which roles.

The data obtained from a beliefs matrix are termed "distributional similarity" data since the similarity of pairs of row items is assessed in terms of the degree of match of their yes/no responses across all the column items;

that is, the manner in which the set of responses for the row items *distributes* across the column items, and vice versa. For these data, in other words, the similarity of each combination of two roles is based on the amount of agreement in the pattern of yes/no responses the respondent provides when asked whether each activity is done by each role. The distributional similarity of activities is calculated in like manner.

Ninety-two Ixil and 74 Ladinos completed the $R \times A$ matrix. For details on the sample, see Harding 1973. The individual matrices for each ethnic group were aggregated and the similarity of each of the 1225 possible pairs of roles was calculated in terms of their patterns of responses across the 48 activities. The resultant sets of distributional similarity coefficients (0.00 = no similarity, 1.00 = perfect similarity) for the 1225 pairs of roles, taken as a whole, are considered to represent the cognitive structure of roles for each ethnic group. Used as input to multidimensional scaling and hierarchical clustering programs, n-dimensional models of the role structures can be developed. The underlying dimensions of these role structures were then determined through an interpretive analysis of these models as corroborated by ethnographic data. For the Ixil data, a three-dimensional model with a stress of 0.055 was used for analysis; for the Ladino data a three-dimensional model with a stress of 0.070 was used.

3. It should be noted that two individuals might see roles as similar to each other in that both distribute similarly across activities, yet not agree on specific activities with which the roles are associated. Thus, it is possible for there to be agreement on role-role similarity yet disagreement on activity-activity similarity.

4. Judged similarity elicitation data (in contrast to the distributional similarity data, as determined from the beliefs matrix) were also collected from a total of 105 Ixil and 98 Ladinos where informants indicated all the pairs of items they felt were similar out of a list of 15 items. Verbatim responses were collected regarding reasons for similarity.

5. It has been found in past work (see especially Stefflre 1965, 1971) that descriptions of new things "perform" (are reacted to) in "test" situations such as the judged similarity, beliefs matrix, or preference ranking tasks approximately the same way as do names of existing items, and that fairly accurate predictions can be made based on this performance.

6. Two 15-item preference rankings of roles were conducted—the first by 87 Ixil and 55 Ladinos, the second by 90 Ixil and 57 Ladinos.

7. See Clement (1976) for a discussion of information specificity and prediction.

REFERENCES

Bateson, Gregory, 1972. A Theory of Play and Fantasy. In *Steps to an Ecology of the Mind* (New York: Ballentine Books), pp. 177–93.

Black, Mary B., 1974. Belief Systems. In *Handbook of Social and Cultural Anthropology,* John J. Honigmann, ed. (New York: Rand McNally), pp. 509–77.

Blumer, Herbert, 1953. Psychological Import of the Human Group. In

Group Relations at the Crossroads, Muzafer Sherif and M. O. Wilson, eds. (New York: Harper), pp. 199–201.

Buckley, Walter, ed., 1968. *Modern Systems Research for the Behavioral Scientist* (Chicago: Aldine).

Burton, Michael L., 1972. Semantic Dimensions of Occupation Names. In *Multidimensional Scaling: Theory and Applications in the Behavioral Sciences, Vol. II: Applications,* A. K. Romney, Roger N. Shepard, and Sara Beth Nerlove, eds. (New York: Seminar Press), pp. 55–71.

———, and A. Kimbal Romney, 1975. A Multidimensional Representation of Role Terms. *American Ethnologist* 2(3) : 397–407.

Cancian, Francesca, 1975. *What are Norms? A Study of Beliefs and Action in a Maya Community* (Cambridge: Cambridge University Press).

Clement, Dorothy C., 1974. *Samoan Concepts of Mental Illness and Treatment* (Ph.D. diss., University of California, Irvine).

———, 1976. Cognitive Anthropology and Applied Problems in Education. In *Do Applied Anthropologists Apply Anthropoolgy?,* Michael Angrosino, ed. (Athens: University of Georgia Press), pp. 53–71.

———, et al., 1973. *Perceptions of and Preferences for Alternative Living Environments in Santa Clara County: Final Report* (Berkeley, Calif.: Policy Research and Planning Group).

Colby, Benjamin N., 1966. Ethnographic Semantics: A Preliminary Survey. *Current Anthropology* 7: 3–17.

———, and Pierre van den Berghe, 1969. *Ixil Country* (Berkeley: University of California Press).

D'Andrade, Roy G., et al., 1972. Categories of Disease in American English and Mexican-Spanish. In *Multidimensional Scaling: Theory and Applications in the Behavioral Sciences, Vol. II: Applications,* A. K. Romney et al., eds. (New York: Seminar Press), pp. 11–55.

Durbin, Marshall, 1974. Cognitive Anthropology. In *Handbook of Social and Cultural Anthropology,* John J. Honigmann, ed. (New York: Rand Mc-Nally), pp. 447–78.

Goodenough, W. H., 1965. Rethinking "Status" and "Role." In *The Relevance of Models in Social Anthropology,* M. Banton, ed. (New York: Praeger), pp. 1–22.

Gross, Neal, Ward S. Mason, and A. W. McEachern, 1958. *Exploration in Role Analysis* (New York: John Wiley).

Harding, Joe R., 1973. *Cognitive Role Structure and Culture Contact: Culture Change in the Ixil Region of Guatemala* (Ph.D. diss., University of California, Irvine).

———, 1974. Heuristic Elicitation Methodology and FRM Acceptability. Paper presented to WHO Methodology Conference of the Task Force on the Acceptability of Fertility Regulating Methods, Geneva, Switzerland.

———, and J. Boyer, 1976. *Determination of Zuni Perceptions of Otitis Media Treatments and Attributes: A Methodology and Some Pilot Results* (Report). (Chapel Hill, N.C.: Policy Research and Planning Group.)

———, Dorothy C. Clement, and Kathleen Lammers, 1972. *Perceptions of and Attitudes toward Alternative Living Environments in Santa Clara County* (Report). (Berkeley, Calif.: Policy Research and Planning Group).

———, 1973. *An Architectural Planning Study: Prospective User Perceptions (Form and Functions) of the Proposed Ramah Navajo Learning*

Center (Report). (Berkeley, Calif.: Policy Research and Planning Group).

Landy, David, 1974. Role Adaptation: Traditional Curers under the Impact of Western Medicine. *American Ethnologist* 1(1): 103–26.

Lincoln, Jackson Steward, 1945. *An Ethnological Study of the Ixil Indians of the Guatemala Highlands.* University of Chicago Microfilm Collection. (Chicago: University of Chicago).

Metzger, Duane, 1973. Semantic Procedures for the Study of Belief Systems. In *Drinking Patterns in Highland Chiapas,* Henning Siverts, ed. (Bergen, Norway: Universitetsforlaget), pp. 37–48.

Rappaport, Roy A., 1971a. Ritual, Sanctity and Cybernetics. *American Anthropologist* 73: 45–58.

————, 1971b. The Sacred in Human Evolution. *Annual Review of Ecology and Systematics* 2: 23–44.

————, 1974. Maladaptation in Social Systems. (Paper presented at Department of Anthropology colloquium, University of North Carolina.)

Secord, Paul F., and Carl W. Backman, 1961. Personality Theory and the Problem of Stability and Change in Individual Behavior: An Interpersonal Approach. *Psychological Review* 68(1): 21–32.

Smith, A. L., and Alfred V. Kidder, 1951. *Excavation at Nebaj.* Carnegie Institution Publication 594. (Washington, D.C.: Carnegie Institute).

Stefflre, Volney J., 1965. Simulation of People's Behavior toward New Objects and Events. *The American Behavioral Scientist* 8(9): 12–16.

————, 1972. Some Applications of Multidimensional Scaling to Social Science Problems. In *Multidimensional Scaling: Theory and Applications in the Behavioral Sciences, Vol. II: Applications,* A. Kimball Romney, Roger N. Shepard and Sara Beth Nerlove, eds. (New York: Seminar Press), pp. 211–43.

————, and M. McClaran, 1967. *A Study of the Perception of Peace Corps Volunteers and Their Activities by Spanish and Quechua Speakers in Cuzco and Chimbote, Peru* (Report). (New York: Stefflre Associates).

————, P. Reich, and M. McClaran-Stefflre, 1971. Some Eliciting and Computational Procedures for Descriptive Semantics. In *Explorations in Mathematical Anthropology,* Paul Kay, ed. (Cambridge, Mass.: MIT Press), pp. 79–117.

Strauss, Anselm, et al., 1963. The Hospital and Its Negotiated Order. In *The Hospital in Modern Society,* Eliot Freidson, ed. (New York: Free Press).

Sturtevant, William C., 1964. Studies in Ethnoscience. *American Anthropologist* 6(3) pt. 2, Special Publication, pp. 99–131.

Turner, Ralph H., 1962. Role-Taking: Process versus Conformity. In *Human Behavior and Social Processes,* Arnold M. Rose, ed. (Boston: Houghton Mifflin), chap. 2.

Predicting Culture Change in the Restudy Situation: Ireland

ART GALLAHER, JR.

In this chapter I shall examine certain features of the rural Irish kinship system, with special attention paid to the husband/wife dyad. I have narrowed my focus to these two roles[1] to illustrate better an aspect of culture and strategy which I believe offers excellent predictive possibility when working from a conventional qualitative data base. My basic premise quite simply is that in conventional anthropological research those elements of social organization which involve status progression offer an excellent opportunity for the study and the prediction of change. Further, the analysis and prediction of change are both enhanced through a restudy methodology. In this situation the researcher can develop from the occupants of various status positions information about their role expectations and their actual behavior and can compare these reports to the baseline culture of the original study. These data in turn can be compared to data on the expectations of those who are yet to acquire the status. Discrepancies between the role expectations of current occupants and those who are anticipating occupancy should point to the directions of change in the behavior considered appropriate in a given social relationship.

The theoretical paradigm underlying the analysis presented here is a tension management model of functionalism (Moore and Feldman 1962; Moore 1963). This model shares with the more conventional equilibrium model the notion that much of the change in a social system is induced by external pressures and the related view that structural requisites are present and must be maintained for the continuation of any social system. It differs from the equilibrium model of functionalism in that it recognizes internal as well as external stimuli to change. The tension management model thus views internally generated change particularly, though not exclusively, as efforts to manage the tensions which develop when the normative and behavioral patterns in a social system do not coincide. A basic premise underlying the analysis presented here, then, is that the operational codes of the husband/wife dyad must be consistent with the structural requisites necessary for the continuation of the social relationship. Structural requisites in this context refer to the minimal concerns which are left to the husband/wife dyad—for our purposes the division of domestic labor defined around each of these roles (Bell 1965: 109). Implicit in this notion is the identification of strains or problems on the basis of the dyad's ability to manage those concerns. Operational codes on the other hand refer simply to the do's and don'ts of conduct (Bell 1965: 106).

The general strategy will be to develop first the traditional role expectations of married couples at the time of the Arensberg and Kimball study of rural Ireland done in 1932 (1961). This group I shall refer to as the older generation. This will be followed by looking at the same expectations as they are held by those who have entered the relationship more recently, that is from 1955 to 1965. This group will be referred to as the middle generation. I shall then look at the current generation, those young adults who have not yet progressed to husband/wife roles. In each case I shall note the sources of strain[2] in the husband/wife relationship and describe some of the major strategies for managing such strains. We should then be in a position to make some predictions regarding the direction of culture changes.

The ethnographic context within which the data were derived is that of County Clare in Ireland. Briefly, I have made two major research efforts in that area. The first of these came in the mid-1960s when I spent twelve months in Clare doing a culture change study, using the Arensberg and Kimball (1961) materials collected in 1932 as a baseline for analysis. The second effort consisted of six months in the same area in 1971, this time concerned with following up materials on youth subculture generated during the 1960s research. In effect then, my work in Clare constitutes a longitudinal analysis within a longitudinal analysis, a design which has caused an unusually long stretch-out time in the publication of data. For purposes of this paper, the ethnographic present will be designated as 1971.

The primary method for collecting data has been community study, using the parish of Corofin as the main communal frame of reference. This parish, which contains approximately three thousand people, comprises a large part of the area studied previously by Arensberg and Kimball (1961). While I worked mainly in the parish in 1966, an Irish female assistant spent four months in Luogh, a townland some ten miles away that Arensberg and Kimball had included in their earlier study. On my second field trip I was assisted for three months by a female student from Kentucky. In both cases, the assistants were assigned to focus on teen and young-adult populations, with emphasis on females in each of these categories.

The Irish peasant society described by Arensberg and Kimball for 1932 was characterized by a dispersed farm pattern, with subsistence gardening and a mixed cattle economy. Clare is an area of very poor soil, high rainfall, and bog land that is poorly drained. Farms are transmitted to the son of parental choice, with succession a major problem because of the reluctance of the elderly to turn over their land. Partly as a result of this, marriages, which in 1932 were arranged by parents, occurred quite late. Catholic in religion and fiercely nationalistic in their view of the future, the people of Clare, like those of the rest of western Ireland, have given over their sons and daughters to immigration for well over a hundred years. At the time of the Arensberg and Kimball visit, local leadership was vested in senior, successful males, who effectively upheld the value of tradition. The peasantry were, however, targets of an ambitious program by the government to improve their level of living. This program involved a national effort to improve agricultural technology, including mechanization of some labor-intensive tasks, soil improvement, and limited schemes for land redistribution. For those who could not make a living farming, an industrial scheme was developed to create job opportunities in small-scale industries located in villages and towns.

Kindred were reckoned bilaterally, with a patrilineal bias, and a residence group that corresponded roughly to the stem family.[3] In this system, upon marriage a couple assumed patrilocal residence and control of the land, and the groom's aged parents retired to a place of honor in the west room of the farm cottage. In time, of course, three generations would be housed under the same roof. This residential group functioned as the major unit of production and consumption in Irish society.

In this arrangement, the role expectations of a wife included her assuming responsibility for the care and feeding of young stock, especially calves and bonhams (piglets); caring for the chickens; doing the milking; and making the butter. For her labor in these areas, all income derived from the sale of eggs and butter was hers to dispense as she saw fit. In addition, a wife was expected to work alongside her husband in certain farm tasks which were labor-intensive and where time was critical. Of particular importance was saving the hay from the meadow. This activity, which occurs in late July and early August, is a period of great tension when all effort is bent to claim the hay before the weather goes bad. Women therefore pitched, raked, and helped with the haycocks in the fields, while men worked the mowing machines and built the rick in the haggard. In addition women labored with husbands in May to win the all-important turf from the bog. While men did the actual cutting in the bog trenches, their wives kneaded the peat into briquets and piled it for drying (Arensberg and Kimball 1961: 49). Women also helped with the potato crop.

> At the potato planting the women do the arduous work of planting the sprouts which they have prepared, bending over to put them into the ridges prepared by the men. . . . At the potato lifting they go along behind the man who turns the potatoes out of the ridge with spade and plough, and pick them up. (Arensberg and Kimball 1961: 49)

A husband in turn had responsibility for directing all of the work on the farm.

> In his special province he looks after and cares for the cattle, has full control over them, and takes complete charge of buying and selling them. He disposes of the income they bring in. . . . All of the work requiring heavy effort in garden and field falls to his lot. He makes and tends the drains, fences, barns, and shelters, which protect both cattle and garden produce. He works the fields and gardens with plough, mower, harrow, and spade. All the agricultural implements and the heavy work involved in their use and in the use of the horse are his province. (Arensberg and Kimball 1961: 47)

In addition to the farm tasks noted, all domestic and child-care tasks fell to the wife. She ministered to both the physical and emotional needs of the young children while at the same time she prepared and served food, mended clothing, and tended the hearth. Hers was a job that never seemed finished, confining her to home and hearth except for trips to Mass.

Consistent with the point just made, Arensberg and Kimball noted in 1932 (1961: 202–3) that in all social matters outside the home human activity was generally divided into male and female spheres.

> Men and women are much more often to be seen in the company of members of their own sex than otherwise, except in the house itself. Except upon ceremonial occasions in family life or in the considerable afflu-ence of owning a gig or a trap or a motorcar, in Clare at least they go to mass, to town, or to sportive gatherings with companions of their own sex. Till recently and even now in remote districts, a conventional peasant woman always kept several paces behind her man, even if they were walk-ing somewhere together.

Significantly, this social separation of the sexes operated to provide males much greater freedom of movement and provided them ample oppor-tunity to escape the boredom and monotony of routine tasks. They were out to fairs, to hurling matches, and in the long nights of winter they were free to go out on *cuaird*, that is to visit with neighbors. Women did not go on *cuaird*, but rather spent their time in their duties at home.

Arensberg and Kimball also observed that a major function of the family was to impose a rigid formalism on sexual activity (1961: chap. 11). In this system females were expected to be paragons of sexual morality; any impropriety, real or assumed, was dealt with severely. So strong were the moral sanctions that sexual misconduct had the effect literally of "declassing" offenders. Further,

> apart from the moral censure misconduct brings upon a young woman and the shame it inflicts upon the people of her "name," it brings as well the destruction of her social role. It makes an end of her potentialities, for these, too, are her "character": potential motherhood of a familist line on the one hand, and potential transmission of an advantageous alliance on the other. In a familistic order they are identical. (Arensberg and Kimball 1961: 218)

At that time, too, sexual puritanism seemed to be on the increase (1961: 206). In this scheme of behavior, initiation of sexual activity was expected of the male. Procreation, rather than enjoyment, was the major objective.

The standards for behavior which Arensberg and Kimball described reveal a division of domestic and farm labor which produced more severe role constraints on wife than on husband and a system for making decisions which generally subordinated wife to husband. The evidence available from their analysis, confirmed by older-generation respondents who worked with me, reveals that discrepancies between the normative and behavioral in actual social interaction were the exception rather than the rule.

Using the 1932 baseline, my strategy in looking for change in the husband/wife dyad between then and 1971 has been to look first for congruities between normative and behavioral patterns as these existed in the latter year. I discovered quickly that both older and middle generations were familiar with the role expectations delineated by Arensberg and Kimball and, for the most part, recognized them as the appropriate guides which people in their generation ought to have learned for their behavior.

Analysis, however, reveals that both generations are sensitive to what they perceive as the economic, political, and social subordination of wives to husbands. For the wives in particular this is a major source of tension. This subordination occurs in the expectations attached to the role of wife in three major areas of social interaction. The areas are (1) the traditional division of economic labor, which applies mainly to the small farm sector; (2) the social separation of the sexes; and (3) the nonprocreational aspects of sexual activity. Of these three areas, husbands perceive role strain as deriving mainly from the third one.

Older-generation wives currently react negatively to the traditional division of economic farm labor which they have known much of their lives. In so doing they compare their lot unfavorably with that of sisters and daughters who have emigrated. The new images of wife roles communicated by female relatives abroad are reenforced by the efforts of the Irish Country Women's Association and various government development agencies to redefine wife and mother roles. Older-generation wives thus are openly regretful that they have lived their lives relatively isolated on small farms and at a level of living far below that of their relatives in the city.

Material comfort and convenience are values that emerge clearly in their criticisms; they feel deprived not to have been able to participate in more of the material comforts which they know to exist; they point to changes in creamery and commercial poultry production as restricting even their former limited prerogatives in economic decisions. Above all, older-generation wives bemoan the conflict remembered in their roles of mother and farm helper. The following quote from one of them summarizes adequately the feelings of her generation: "Thinking back on it, there was never enough time for the children. The farm work was always there. I never knew anything but the black apron and Wellingtons." In retrospect, it appears that most of these women coped with their role strains largely by ignoring them, that is through compartmentalization (Goode 1960: 486). Their fatalistic acceptance of the conditions, and their long-suffering silence about them, even became virtues in the romanticized notions of the "good life" as it is recalled by so many migrants. There are a few, however, who are critical of their plight and in retrospect wish they had not so passively accepted their roles while younger.

Middle-generation women on the farm sense the same strain as their mothers, and in addition they feel that they should have a more explicit role in economic decisions. A strong element in their dissatisfaction is the stem family household unit in which many still live. Middle-generation wives, particularly, are critical of the constraints on their decision-making prerogatives which they feel in a household dominated by the husband's parents. Unlike their mothers, however, on this score and others, they are agitating now for a redefinition of traditional husband and wife roles. The new role of wife would take her largely out of farm work and would consolidate her activities in child care and homemaking; and, consistent with the wishes of many, should enable her to spend more time with her husband. The new role, intended also to give her a greater part in decision-making activities, is gaining support among middle-generation husbands.

The traditional separation of the sexes in all social activities, so characteristic of Irish male-female relations, remains a source of strain for older- and middle-generation wives. Strain in this area is defined mainly around the wife's restricted freedom of movement and restricted initiative vis-a-vis the husband. The issues here are complicated because they have to do with the very etiquette of husband-wife interpersonal relations. At the root of this is the feeling expressed by many wives that their sparse social involvement is demeaning; they feel ignored, left out. There is resentment that leisure time for them is either poorly defined or does not exist at all, whereas for husbands there are the fairs and the pub and the freedom to come and go at will. They blame the society for not providing more opportunities for social involvement by women, and they are critical of those husbands who are too blind or selfish to be aware of the injustice in their situation.

> The older husbands and wives don't talk to each other. . . . They don't seem able to. . . . He has his freedom so he just goes his way . . . and the wife suffers in silence. You can see it all through this parish. . . . But 'twill change, for sure. The young girls won't accept that kind of treatment.

Women of the older generation, again, manage largely by ignoring the problem, just as the respondent notes in the above quote. Middle-generation wives on the other hand seek to redefine their roles, to expand social freedom and involvement in a wide range of social activities. Even during the period covered by my research, the barrier against a woman accompanying her husband into a local pub has weakened. The attitude persists that to gain this freedom will not only increase contact with husbands but will modify the quality of interaction with them. Younger husbands indicate that this redefinition of roles, which modifies their own expectations of both rights and obligations, is acceptable; older-generation husbands generally profess not to know that there is a problem, or if they do, to define it from their own perspective. The following observation, albeit by a bachelor, is not atypical of older husbands who frequent the pubs:

> Aye, the pub is a great place, altogether. I'm just after a good pint and a chat with the boys. There's women in it now and that will make a big change . . . and not for the better. Sure, the women have been going in the cities and places like Ennis, but 'tis new for Corofin. You'd never know where 'twill all stop. Women should keep together, like.

The source of greatest marital role strain is in the sexual union of husband and wife. In this area there are the usual strains accompanying inhibition and guilt, traceable mainly to socialization experience, especially in matters religious. There are also strains related to the subordination of decision prerogatives of wife to husband, all of which are attributed to Catholic belief. The most significant strain, however, is that deriving from the conflicting values the partners bring into their sexual encounter. Put simply, the common view of husbands that sexual contact should lead to physical satisfaction conflicts with the view of many wives that such interaction should be based on emotional and affective ties. The issue for the wife clearly is one of being desired. The strength of this redefinition of a basic element in the husband-wife relationship should not be underestimated, and undoubtedly it is a major factor in the precipitous decline of, and negative value placed on, arranged marriages. Arensberg and Kimball (1961: 107) referred to the latter in 1932 as:

> the nearly universal form of marriage in the Irish countryside. . . . It is a central focus of rural life, a universal turning point in individual histories. This form of marriage is known as matchmaking. It is the usual, in fact until recently the only respectable, method of marriage and usually too of inheritance.

Today, the "made match" is so rare as to be an oddity. Middle- and current-generation males and females alike stress the values of love and personal choice as the foundation for courtship and marriage. In other aspects of her relationship to husband the middle-generation wife in particular insists on greater equity and emotional consolidation with him, seeking especially to involve husbands in the care of young children.

All evidence points to inadequate management of role strain in the area of physical sex. The implications are doubly significant because Catholic norms do not permit divorce. Since this option is not available, other adaptive strategies must be developed. The one invoked most often is that of limited role disengagement. Husband or wife, for example, takes another bed, and verbal and physical interaction virtually cease. This tactic, also commonly used in other types of marital dispute, can lead to bizarre consequences. Husband and wife may live in the same house for months on end, but by word and deed each may virtually ignore the other's presence.

In this situation, a strategy of limited disengagement does not, of course, solve the role strain of either of the parties. This tactic, in fact, combined with the inability of the conflicting parties to communicate their perception of a problem to each other, can escalate strain to the point where the disengagement is compounded. There is, for example, "divorce Irish style" (Rohan 1969: 50), where one of the parties simply moves away, maybe to England or perhaps to Dublin, and in extreme cases is not heard from again. This pattern, though occurring more frequently in urban than in rural places, is becoming more common in Corofin and surrounding areas.

The above patterns indicated to me that older and middle generations share the same or similar concerns for the role of the wife and that the behavior of many middle-generation husbands and wives is at variance with traditional expectations. I then formulated questions to be asked of the current generation in the society. These were in the form of a questionnaire and interview schedule administered to 98 girls and 63 boys, the total population in the nearest rural-based academic and vocational secondary schools, in the adjoining parish of Ennistymon. In addition, interviews of several hours each were conducted with 25 percent of the population just noted and with other teenaged youngsters not part of the secondary school population.

Eighty-nine percent of the young people consulted indicated a preference for marriage over bachelorhood or spinsterhood. When placed in the context of the Irish small farm, however, 55 percent of the girls rejected outright the notion of marrying a small farmer, with an additional 34 percent so qualifying their response as to virtually exclude the possibility. Over half of the boys consulted indicated they felt that a small farmer would have greater difficulty securing a wife than would men in other occupations.

The responses of both boys and girls to questions requesting them to project idealized role models for husband and wife on the small farm, expresses clearly their rejection of those role attributes defined as stressful by the older and middle generations. There is general agreement, for example, that the woman's contribution to agricultural tasks has to be redefined; agreement is high that the economic and social milieu of the farm wife is too restrictive. It is consistent with these responses that girls stress heavily the need to have a satisfactory personal relationship with their husbands, one of strong mutual respect and reciprocity; they advocate a nuclear household as opposed to the more traditional stem family. Love and personal choice are expressed as desirable criteria for engaging marriage, leading both boys and girls to reject completely the pattern of arranged matches. In fact, many in the current generation confess ignorance of how the older system worked. Regarding current-generation attitudes on husband-wife roles, only one in four girls had sought advice directly from their mothers, while one in seven boys had. Only one in fifteen respondents had sought such advice from fathers. It is interesting that virtually all current-generation respondents can confirm parental attitudes regarding husband-wife roles on the small farm.

Enough has been said to make the point that those who have not yet married are identifying the same points of tension in the expectations attached to husband-wife roles as the older and middle generations who are already interacting with these expectations. Based on the concerns thus documented over three generations, it seems reasonable to make some modest predictions. These are based on the fact that the older married generation handled its role strain largely through compartmentalization, while middle-generation spouses are modifying their behavior and at the same time insisting on a redefinition of the standards. Those still unmarried, on the other hand, show strong reluctance to do so unless the standards are changed. To reaffirm a basic premise stated earlier: The operational codes of the husband/wife dyad must be made consistent with the structural requisites necessary for the continuation of the social relationship. In order for the society to achieve the latter, I predict therefore that within the next generation:

1. The nuclear household will replace the stem family household as the expected residence pattern for those engaging husband-wife roles. This is a direct response to the middle-generation concern for greater involvement in domestic decision making, especially by wives. Current-generation females and males recognize the need for this autonomy and delineate this as one of the major issues in arriving at a satisfactory marriage.
2. A democratic decision-making model will govern the family's decisions, such as economic expenditures, care of children, sexual relationships, the use of leisure time, and related matters. This is in direct response to the older- and middle-generation concerns for modifying the current subordination of women in the decision-making process. These changes primarily affect the husband/wife dyad. Those indicated in number one above involve stem family relatives.
3. The standards for dividing labor within the farm household will lead to greater dichotomization of economic work roles between husbands and wives. This relates directly to the concern expressed by all generations that women must give over farm labor in favor of mother and affective wife roles.

Finally, I wish to make a few observations regarding restudy methodology and its place in predicting sociocultural change from a qualitative base. As Oscar Lewis (1953: 469) observes, this method minimizes one of the greatest problems in the analysis of culture change, namely, the difficulty of establishing an accurate baseline from which change can be measured. By extension, this advantage is also applicable to the problem of predicting culture change. In short, the restudy provides greater, more precise control over not only baseline but also time depth. This is greater control than one can expect from the conventional one-time field situation. This improved control is useful in making predictions because it enables more accurate judgment about trends than one is likely to get through historical sources or by asking respondents to reconstruct the past from memory.

The restudy offers a second advantage: it provides greater insight into whether the variables prompting change are internally or externally derived. My view on this matter is that the external conditions to which a culture must adapt are themselves always subject to fluctuation in their own right. Our chances for predicting culture change, therefore, are greater in those areas where we can deal with internal variables, discounting accident, of course. The baseline data provided by a restudy should enable one, then, to excise internal variables more easily than would be possible when constructing them through conventional historical sources or, again, through resorting to respondent reconstructions of the past.

NOTES

1. By "role" I am referring to the set of expectations applied to an incumbent of a particular position. Because of the many conceptual distinctions drawn around "role," in this paper I shall usually refer to "role expectations."

2. "Role strain" refers to felt inadequacy, namely the difficulty in meeting given role demands, expressed by the incumbent in a given position. I adhere to Goode's (1960) position that one cannot meet all of one's role expectations to the satisfaction of all persons who are part of one's total role network. Role strain therefore is to be viewed as normal. Viewed another way, an individual's total role obligations are always over-demanding.

3. A stem family is a family comprising two or more nuclear units, each at a different generation level.

REFERENCES

Arensberg, Conrad, and Solon T. Kimball, 1961. *Family and Community in Ireland* (Gloucester, Mass.: Peter Smith).

Bell, Daniel, 1965. Twelve Modes of Prediction. In *Penguin Survey of the Social Sciences 1965,* Julius Gold, ed. (Baltimore, Md.: Penguin Books), pp. 96–127.

Goode, William J., 1960. A Theory of Role Strain. *American Sociological Review* 25: 483–96.

Lewis, Oscar, 1953. Controls and Experiments in Field Work. In *Anthropology Today: An Encyclopedic Inventory,* A. L. Kroeber, ed. (Chicago: University of Chicago Press), pp. 452–75.

Moore, Wilbert, 1963. *Social Change* (New York: Prentice-Hall).

————, and Arnold Feldman, 1962. Society as a Tension-management System. In *Behavioral Science and Civil Defense Disaster Research Group, Study Number 16,* George Baker and Leonard Cottrell, Jr., eds. (Washington: National Academy of Sciences, National Research Council), chap. 8.

Rohan, Dorine, 1969. *Marriage Irish Style* (Cork: Mercier Press).

The Use of Computer Simulation Models for Predicting Sociocultural Change

BONNIE A. NARDI

This paper seeks to describe the computer simulation technique as it is used in anthropology and to assess the degree to which it may be useful for predicting sociocultural change. A computer simulation model shares with other types of models the goal of providing the investigator with a simplified analogy for some natural phenomenon for the purpose of better analyzing and understanding that phenomenon. It differs from other types of models in that it focuses on conducting experiments on a computer in which mathematical or logical operations describing the behavior of a system over time are of primary importance. A simulation model enables the investigator to experiment by changing values of the variables in the model and to concentrate on tracking changes over time in the model of interest. Its very purpose, in fact, is the analysis of change over time.

Computer simulation is a powerful technique, capable of handling large numbers of variables representing complex systems and of simulating the operation of these variables over many cycles, but it is immediately limited by the investigator's prior understanding of the system to be modeled, and the development of a useful model demands strong empirical underpinnings. For a well-defined, relatively well understood system, the simulation technique offers a means of determining the *direction* and *rate of change* of individual variables in the system and the system as a whole within specifiable limits.

It gives the investigator a chance experimentally to test hypotheses about the logical outcomes of a set of conditions said to characterize a system by playing out the variables in the system as they change over time. The technique is oriented toward modeling entire systems which encompass a broad holistic framework incorporating many variables and variables of different types. A computer simulation model is as fully capable of handling a residence rule specifying matrilocal residence in the case of marriage to the mother's brother's daughter's son as it is capable of keeping track of the number of yams accumulated by the headman of a tropical village. It allows the investigator to generate, remember, and record large numbers of transactions and operations for as long a period as is desired.

In this paper I will describe the application of the simulation technique to anthropological problems and evaluate its potentialities and limitations for studying problems of sociocultural change. Data from my computer simulation model of exogamous marriage in small populations are used to illustrate some of the points in the paper. Throughout I stress the appropriateness of the simulation technique for anthropologists studying change.

DESCRIPTION OF THE SIMULATION TECHNIQUE

Computer simulation models were first developed by engineers simulating the behavior of highly specifiable mechanical systems. Such models were developed to answer questions about systems characterized by series of simultaneous nonlinear equations for which only simulation solutions are available (Tustin 1968: 73). Anthropologists using simulation techniques agree that analytic models of cultural systems incorporating even simple social processes require extremely sophisticated mathematical techniques which are not within the grasp of many anthropologists. In many cases, on the other hand, analytic techniques may not be adequate for incorporating social processes which would be of interest to an anthropologist (see Johnston and Albers 1973: 206; MacCluer 1973: 222; Hammel and Wachter 1975; Wobst 1975: 76 on this point). Computer simulation models are appropriate in a variety of contexts in which relationships between variables are believed to be complex and where analytic models have not been developed.

Simulation models allow for systematic study of sociocultural processes wherein the effects of changes in various parameters in the total system can be examined with some precision. Simulation modeling demands an explicit presentation of a conception of a total system, and a simulation model of a cultural system is, in a sense, a formal description of that system. It is the first (and most difficult) task of the anthropologist to specify the system as he or she sees it, including in the development of the model both the identification of the variables which belong in the model and the rates, equations, or operations which characterize the behavior of variables in the model.

Specifying a system is a risky and often highly arbitrary venture. Friedenberg, a systems theorist, describes a system simply as an "arbitrary segment of the world about us" (Friedenberg 1968). The *Oxford En-*

glish Dictionary tells us that a system is neither small, simple nor partial. It defines a system as "a set or assemblage of things connected, associated, or interdependent, so as to form a complex unity; a whole composed of parts in orderly arrangement according to some scheme or plan; rarely applied to a simple or small assemblage of things" (*OED* 1971: 393). The system concept is most useful in stressing the interdependent nature of variables which an investigator can circumscribe and study. A system is typically taken to involve a *set of elements* and their *interrelations*. The set may consist of "abstract entities, real objects, beliefs, ideas, . . . or any conceivable kind of being; the important thing is that this set be, to some better than random degree, an articulated set, one whose behavior can be seen to present some patterned sequence to an observer" (Darrouzet 1976: 1–2).

To anthropologists, trained in the holistic tradition, conceptualizing a culture or subculture as a system is not very remarkable and fits naturally into the anthropological perspective, which stresses the essential unity and interconnectedness of the cultural phenomena labeled kinship, religion, politics, etc. However, in moving beyond a qualitative description of a system (such as a traditional ethnography) toward an effort to analyze precisely relationships between the various types of cultural phenomena with an eye to predicting change, it becomes necessary to concentrate a great deal of effort on the study of the relationships themselves. This involves specifying the effects that changes of one variable in the system are expected to have on others and in some cases quantifying the changes. The study of sociocultural change presents exciting possibilities for the study of cultural systems. It is only by virtue of an observable change in one parameter that we can isolate the relationships between various types of cultural phenomena by observing the changes produced in other areas of the system. Without change, an institution or belief (or whatever) remains an environmental constant, and its effects on other aspects of the sociocultural system will go undetected because it cannot manifest change.

The second task of the investigator devising a computer simulation model is to specify, quantitatively if need be, the relationship between parameters in the model. The technique demands that explicit decisions be made regarding the operation of variables in the model.

The two tasks taken together require first an insightful choice of the variables which are crucial to the problem at hand and, second, strict specification of the operation of the variables identified as belonging to the system. The investigator seeks to define the problem exhaustively, but in its essentials only, and to arrive at an explicit and thorough description of the system, which is then translated into a set of computer instructions and run on the computer.

Given the complexity of sociocultural phenomena, it is almost impossible to specify strictly the many operations required to simulate a sociocultural process. However, the capabilities of the computer leave open the possibility of varying parameters when exact values are established for different sets of conditions. The investigator therefore generates a series of predictions which can be evaluated according to which set of conditions seems most probable.

The investigator can also simulate stochastic variation[1] or patterned variation depending upon which is more appropriate. Given a set of initial conditions he or she generates not one outcome but a series of outcomes with varying probabilities.

Once the basic decisions about the model have been made and it has been translated into computer instructions, the investigator puts the model through many runs, each with many cycles in order to observe the changes in the system. Cycles can be days, years, generations, etc., but these serve to move the system forward through time, while the system accumulates the changes in which the investigator is interested. It can be stopped after any number of cycles so that they can be compared over time.

Because it becomes immediately apparent that the number of possibilities for parameter variation is large, it is helpful to be working with a series of hypotheses about the system, and a definite theoretical framework. This becomes critical in analyzing what can quickly amount to masses of data output by the computer.

In analyzing the data, the investigator attempts to center efforts on establishing the direction and rates of change suggested by the runs of the simulation model and to assess their implications for states of the system at various times (including future times). The implications may be of a quantitative or qualitative nature.

A COMPUTER SIMULATION MODEL OF
LINEAGE EXOGAMY IN SMALL POPULATIONS

Because I will be discussing my computer simulation model (Nardi 1977) throughout the rest of the paper to provide an example of the use of simulation in anthropology, I will describe the model briefly here. The model was not devised to study a problem in the prediction of sociocultural change; it was used to examine change in the past and deals with problems of prehistory. The development and operation of a computer simulation model for predicting sociocultural change, however, would be essentially the same.

The model of lineage exogamy concerned the nature of social organization in hunting-gathering societies. There are two schools of thought on this subject. Some anthropologists argue that hunter-gatherers maintain strict lineal groupings with exogamy rules restricting marriage partners (Radcliffe-Brown 1930; Service 1962; Birdsell 1970; Williams 1974; Martin 1975). Others hold that hunter-gatherers are organized into fluid, flexible groupings with shifting alliances and membership in groups (Hiatt 1966; Turnbull 1968; Lee and DeVore 1968; Steward 1968; Peterson 1975). A flexible organization provides hunter-gatherers numerous advantages, including conflict resolution, leveling of demographic variance, and efficient utilization of resources. An organization of rigidly defined groups, furthermore, is not feasible given the small population size, low rate of population growth, and stochastic fluctuation in demographic parameters characteristic of such groups. In particular, restrictive marriage rules (lineage exogamy) and demographic variation would decrease the supply of marriage partners to the point where reproduction would decrease (assuming that only married people reproduce).

The computer simulation model was designed to assess the last proposition. Do demographic constraints restrict the development and maintenance of lineal groupings in hunting-gathering communities? In order to test this hypothesis a computer simulation was designed to simulate social and demographic processes in a model population. Demographic parameters were used that most closely estimate those of the hunting-gathering groups studied by anthropologists. The social organization modeled was that of a multi-lineage society characterized by matrilineality, lineage exogamy, limited polygyny, and merging and splitting of lineages.

Two sets of computer runs were done: one which included polygyny and one which did not. The results of the simulation revealed that lineage organization was not constrained by small population size, low rate of population growth, and stochastic fluctuation, as long as the operation of limited polygyny was included in the model. Runs with polygyny showed a stable population that maintained itself over time, but runs without polygyny showed a declining population. Since polygyny or some functional equivalent such as extramarital reproduction, adoption, etc., would be likely to be operative in hunting-gathering groups, it was concluded that lineage organization is demographically feasible in such populations.

USES OF COMPUTER SIMULATION FOR PREDICTING SOCIOCULTURAL CHANGE

In terms of predicting sociocultural change, one of the key advantages of simulation is that it allows the investigator to assess the degree to which a change in a sociocultural system will affect that system. In terms of predicting and planning for change, it is highly useful to know *how much* change to expect. Because a simulation model incorporates both quantitative as well as qualitative relationships, the investigator modeling a problem of sociocultural change can expect the model to generate quantitative data indicating the degree of change to be expected. Again it should be noted that a prior insightful understanding of the system is necessary for deriving a reasonable model. But once the investigator has produced a defensible model, the computer is useful for generating and compiling a large number of interactions to determine the likely outcome of the changes occurring in the model.

With my model I was interested in examining relationships between rules of lineage exogamy, random variation, lineage maintenance, and population size. Since the individual was the smallest unit in the simulation, every individual in the model was followed over time, and events of the individual's life were calculated and recorded. Changes in lineages and in the total population were a function of the events which happened to individuals. The model thus embodied thousands of individual interactions which could be tracked and recorded only because of the computer.

I concluded that adherence to rules of lineage exogamy is possible in the context of the demographic conditions associated with primitive populations. Changes in the number of individuals in the population were negligible for the polygynous populations and were due to random variation and not to the effects of restrictive marriage rules. However, in nonpolygynous populations, observance of the restrictive marriage rule did lead to change—a declining population. The running of the model therefore allowed me to identify conditions under which one might expect change and to determine how much change to expect. Rates of change can be seen in Figure 1, which shows population size over time in polygynous and nonpolygynous populations.

Assessing the degree to which a change in a sociocultural system will affect that system may be particularly critical in cases where those changes appearing to be small changes at the micro-level can be demonstrated to have large systemic effects.

Anthropological sensibilities attend to the relationship of the individ-

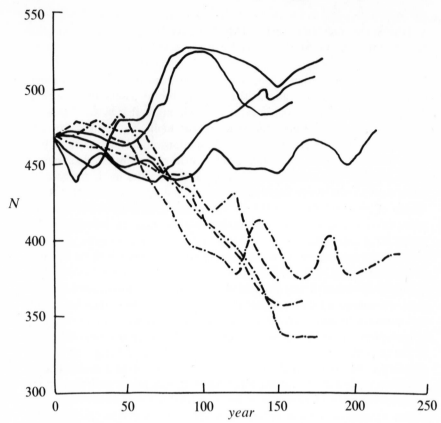

Figure 1. Population Size in Four Populations with Polygyny (————),
and Four Populations without Polygyny (– · – · – · – · –).

ual and society and thus accommodate a perspective which heeds the
importance of the cumulative effects of individual behaviors for a total
system. Simulation modeling seems to be an appropriate tool for anthropologists concerned with change, as it allows for coupling an awareness
of the relationship of the one and the many with a systematized method
of dealing with such relationships. Use of simulation modeling to test
the effects of "small" individual behaviors on the total system provides
the anthropologist with a method for demonstrating the degree to which
large system-wide effects are likely to ensue from small changes and to
produce clear and explicit reasons why.

There are at least two types of situations in which we observe "small"
changes to have system-wide repercussions. One situation is that of the
overall, aggregated effects of many individual behaviors, for example the

air pollution caused by hundreds of thousands of three-quarter-mile automobile trips to the grocery. Another instance in which we may expect "small" changes to have system-wide effects is through "reverberation effects"—that is, when a change in one variable affects other variables throughout the system by virtue of the fact that they stand linked together in an interdependent fashion rather than standing as isolated entities. These types of changes are not confined to linear chain reaction effects but also include interactive changes such as feedback effects and multivariate causal links.

If one accepts the interconnectedness of sociocultural phenomena it seems obvious that even a small change in one sphere, such as the introduction of a new crop, may affect the entire sociocultural system. It is surprising, however, how often we overlook the potential effects of such changes and fail to predict outcomes which seem in retrospect altogether too predictable.

This is really as much a problem of expecting and looking for such changes as of quantifying their effects, but the use of a simulation model may help to demonstrate the manner in which such phenomena operate. Again, the degree to which such changes affect a system may be studied and analyzed by means of a computer simulation model.

Simulation models are also useful for ascertaining the point at which a change will make a difference in a system; that is, it is a way of pinpointing a threshold effect, or the "difference that makes a difference." This is a special case, but an especially important one, of assessing the degree to which a change in a sociocultural system will affect other areas of the system. A system will usually tolerate some level of variability before exhibiting significant change of a quantitative or qualitative nature. In terms of prediction, it is crucial to know how much variability is withstood before major transformations of the system occur.

In my model of lineage exogamy I did two sets of runs, one which included polygyny and one which did not. The polygynous marriage rule was very limited, allowing only for polygynous marriage of widows to lineage brothers of their dead husband, and a husband could not be married to more than two wives at any one time. Polygyny was tested as a homeostatic device (maintaining stability and survival of the population) since it is a practice widely associated with lineage systems and involves a very simple modification of rules in a social system, as has been suggested by Kunstadter (1973) and MacCluer and Dyke (1973).

Analysis of the data from the simulation runs revealed that the polygynous populations were stationary over time while the nonpolygynous populations declined (see figure 1). Populations with polygyny offered a sufficiently large supply of marriage partners to women of reproductive age to maintain universal marriage for these women, while non-polygynous populations did not.

In polygynous populations there was no variance at all in the proportion of women of reproductive age married. In nonpolygynous populations the proportion of married women did vary. However, the average proportion of unmarried women of reproductive age,

$$\frac{\text{number of unmarried women}}{\text{total number of women}},$$

was only .036. Even this small proportion of women prevented from reproducing led to declining populations in the context of a zero growth rate and small population size. Therefore the addition to the model of one social rule which did not affect large numbers of individuals made the difference between the "life and death" of the entire model population. Incorporation of the rule of limited polygyny into the marriage system controlled population decline and thereby made possible the survival of the population.

In this instance a rather small amount of variability had important systemic effects; in fact it affected the very survival of the system. Few individuals in the model population were affected, but the changes accruing to those few were the difference that makes a difference in this case.

Simulation modeling is capable of exploiting another anthropological propensity—that which emphasizes description. Anthropologists endeavor to describe cultures, subcultures, and sociocultural systems, with thoroughgoing and wide-ranging holism. Such descriptions may be considered as a series of propositions appertaining to a system in that statements about a culture can be analyzed for implications they have for the culture. The logical outcomes of the transactions and operations over time of the phenomena contained in the propositions can be modeled and tested via simulation. This is a way of evaluating the value of the description and suggesting ways in which it may be modified and improved. It can also be a way of evaluating competing descriptions of the same system. That is, if X, Y, and Z characterize the system proposed by A, what are the consequences of X, Y, and Z's operating after a period of years? The description of B may be evaluated similarly.

One of the purposes of the computer model of lineage systems that I constructed was to evaluate two conflicting descriptive models of hunter-gatherer social organization. Analysis of the models with the quantitative data provided by the simulation provides support for one model and demonstrates the way descriptive and quantitative models may complement one another.

One of the first examples of the traditional model of hunter-gatherer social organization is Radcliffe-Brown's description of the Australian horde:

> Therefore, as a normal thing, male members enter the horde by birth and remain in it till death. In many regions the horde is exogamous. . . . The horde, therefore, as an existing group at any moment, consists of (1) male members of all ages, whose fathers and fathers' fathers belonged to the horde, (2) unmarried girls who are the sisters or daughters, or sons' daughters of the male members, (3) married women, all of whom, in some regions, and most of whom in others, belonged originally to other hordes, and have become attached to the horde by marriage (Radcliffe-Brown 1930: 35).

This brief paragraph was meant to offer a compact ethnographic description of the essential features of the social organization of the Australian tribes, based on Radcliffe-Brown's extensive fieldwork with the aborigines in northwestern Australia. It soon transcended this relatively modest objective by becoming the dominant model of the social organization of hunting-gathering society. Radcliffe-Brown's somewhat baroque use of the term "horde" was replaced by "band," but the main elements of the description provided the foundation for a model of hunting-gathering society with such proponents as Steward (1936), Service (1962), Birdsell (1970), Williams (1974), and Martin (1975).

Radcliffe-Brown's descriptions of Australian social organization emphasized patrilineality, exogamy, patrilocality. These features remained an essential part of the anthropological description of hunter-gatherer society until they were challenged by Elkin (1950), Meggitt (1962), Hiatt (1966), and others whose own Australian field data showed considerable variation away from the standard patrilineal, patrilocal, exogamous band model. These anthropologists were followed by others who questioned the whole notion of a patrilineal, patrilocal, exogamous band and who formulated an alternative "flux model" of hunting-gathering social organization. They claimed that in many cases a fluid, flexible set of individuals with various kin and non-kin relationships to each other comprised the hunter-gatherer band, instead of its being composed of a single patrilineage. Neither patrilocality nor band exogamy was considered an essential feature of hunting-gathering life (Hiatt 1966; Turnbull 1968; Lee and DeVore 1968; Steward 1968; Peterson 1975).

Proponents of the flux model have criticized the patrilineal-patrilocal band model on the grounds that demographic conditions in hunting-gathering societies would be unlikely to support a social system based on strict rules of descent, residence, and exogamy. Very small groups of people experiencing normal demographic variance in sex ratio, family size, and survivorship would not likely sustain social groups which prescribe patrilocality, patrilineality, and band exogamy. The low rates of growth characteristic of foraging groups would further tend to suggest that a flexible social organization would provide advantages over one based on highly specified group affiliation.

It is assumed by those advocating the flux model that the demography of hunting-gathering groups is inconsistent with a patrilineal/patrilocal band organization. Lee and DeVore (1968) criticized the inflexibility inherent in the lineal band model, noting that "the model leaves scant room either for local and seasonal variations in food supply or for variance in sex ratios and family size within and between local groups" (Lee and DeVore 1968: 9). Anderson (1968) asserted the importance of "chance demographic factors" in determining hunting-gathering social organization, distinct from the more patterned and predictable "local and seasonal variations" mentioned by Lee and DeVore.

Steward's comments on the demographic argument are perhaps the most precise and specific though offered at the level of assertion as the others are. He pointed out some of the key variables which are part of the demographic argument, i.e., band size and number of potential marriage partners. Steward observed, "Owing to expectable fluctuations in the size of primary bands, a strongly patterned cultural ideal of band composition would be difficult to maintain. . . . Composition of the primary band therefore varies, although its core is a number of intermarried families" (Steward 1968: 331).

Data from my model do not support the contention of advocates of the flux model that demographic constraints prevent the formation and maintenance of exogamous lineages in hunting-gathering cultures. Populations with polygyny were entirely stable. Although it could be argued that hunting-gathering groups lacking polygyny might decline, it seems more reasonable to interpret polygyny as one of many possible flexibility-inducing mechanisms that could be called into play if there were other good reasons for sustaining lineage organization.

These other mechanisms would include extramarital reproduction, adoption, exchange of personnel between lineages, or rule breaking. Polygyny is one of many simple modifications which could be incorporated into a system to allow the system to maintain itself without larger structural changes.

It could also be argued that rules establishing lineage affiliations are in fact symbolic and are not frequently followed, so that hunting-gathering groups are not really characterized by a lineage organization. This is entirely possible, but it is then inconsistent with the argument set forth by proponents of the flux model that demographic constraints *prevent* a true lineage-based kinship and marriage system. The results of the computer model suggest that the model arguing that demographic constraints would restrict lineage maintenance in hunting-gathering groups requires reevaluation with respect to that assumption. In addition, these results suggest that other lines of argument in support of the flux model must be put forth by its proponents.

ADVANTAGES OF THE SIMULATION TECHNIQUE

Some of the uses to which computer simulation may be put for the purpose of predicting sociocultural change include assessing the degree to which changes in a sociocultural system affect the total system, ascertaining the impact of "small" individual behaviors in the aggregate, accounting for system-wide "reverberations" of apparently insignificant variations, pinpointing threshold effects, and testing the logical outcomes of a set of propositions about a system. In addition, the simulation approach tends to urge the investigator toward precision, clarity, and completeness. These properties of simulation modeling are discussed below.

The simulation technique obligates the investigator to work with precision and clarity. Simulating a total system involves making decisions about what the system really should look like. These decisions are embodied in the computer program, and even assumptions that might otherwise go unstated are necessarily made manifest by the demands of the program. The necessity of writing instructions to the computer requires unambiguous specification of all aspects of the system to be modeled. The explicitness and clarity demanded by the computer program aid the investigator in developing and presenting a well-formulated, fully articulated model. The model is also amenable to evaluation and criticism by others on all levels from the inclusion of specific variables (and exclusion of others) to the values assigned each variable.

A good understanding of the sociocultural system to be modeled is required for simulation. The investigator may therefore be led to ask useful questions which will further that understanding by the very attempt to describe the system fully. This type of recursion is characteristic of many approaches but seems to be especially encouraged by the simulation technique, again because of the explicitness demanded by the computer program and because of the necessity to include all of the crucial variables and linkages in a system.

Attempts to describe a sociocultural system for purposes of simulation modeling will inevitably suggest many kinds of data that would be useful to collect. Because a good simulation model demands empirical specificity and is focused and problem-oriented, it tends to encourage the investigator to carefully enumerate the types of data which would be useful for establishing a tenable model. It also makes clear the limits of the extant data and the degree to which they can be profitably utilized.

LIMITATIONS OF THE SIMULATION TECHNIQUE

The chief limitation of the simulation technique has been mentioned: a creditable model requires much prior knowledge and must be supported by a firm empirical foundation. The anthropologist should have sound intuitions (hypotheses, theories) about what variables play a part in the system and how the variables stand in relation to one another. This requires making strong assumptions about a problem and limiting the model to those variables believed to be key ones. Inclusion of superfluous variables which do not play an essential role in the operation of the system complicates the model and obfuscates the actual relationships of interest. On the other hand, the anthropologist is always faced with the problem of incompletely describing the system and omitting critical variables. If these problems are not to prevent the construction of a well-grounded model, prior analyses of the problem elucidating its primary elements must be available to the investigator. In addition, some of the variables may require mathematical or statistical measurements, and these data must also be available.

Other limitations of computer modeling are of a more practical nature: computer simulation requires time and money which may not be available to the anthropologist. I have stressed that simulation is an especially apt technique for scholars whose training has emphasized a holistic perspective and who are given to describing things in their perceived entirety. Many anthropologists have not, however, acquired skill in computer science, and in this sense simulation modeling does not work its way effortlessly into the anthropological repertoire. The anthropologist must invest time in learning aspects of computer science or buy an expert's skill and knowledge. Once designed and programmed, the simulation model must of course be run and computer time must be bought for this purpose.

THE UTILIZATION OF COMPUTER SIMULATION MODELS AND SOCIAL POLICY

The simulation models of economists, demographers, and systems analysts are being used more and more frequently in the planning profession, from the local and regional level to global analyses that attempt to model the entire world as a closed system. The recent world models— World Dynamics model (Forrester 1971), The Limits to Growth model (Meadows et al. 1972), and Models of Doom (Cole et al. 1973)—have received worldwide attention and have had tremendous appeal for a wide public. It is difficult to judge their actual impact upon social policy, but their influence on the ubiquitous neo-Malthusian notions embodied in the current concern with overpopulation and environmental decline is unmistakable (Jahoda 1973: 209). Other less well known computer simulation models have been developed by the International Bank for Reconstruction and Development, the International Labour Organization, the United States Commission on Population Growth and the American Future, and the East Pakistan Land and Water Resources Study. These models have received less publicity than the world models mentioned above but have perhaps more immediate potential for influencing policy, since they were conceived specifically as aids to policy formulation within the context of national and international organizations with well-defined economic and political aims.

Anthropologists who are concerned with influencing social policy, in particular policies which aspire to affect the course of economic development in any of its aspects—social, technical, political, environmental —may find it useful to familiarize themselves with computer simulation models currently in use. They may also hope to contribute to future models or to create alternative models.

As the simulation models now stand, they could benefit from anthropological input in several ways. First of all, current computer simulation models suffer from being seriously underspecified (Carter 1975; Cole et al. 1973). They are underspecified both in terms of the types of variables included and in terms of the empirical basis for delineating relationships between variables in the models.

Few of the models have a well-developed sociological component. They are instead confined to variables which represent only population, economy, and environment. Social structural variables are lacking, and even the effects of such processes as the development and utilization of new technologies or the introduction of the "appropriate" technologies into new areas have not been modeled. One simulation model being developed by the International Labour Organization has, however, attempted to incorporate some social variables—for example, demand for education—to predict the track of economic development in Third World countries. Conceptual and theoretical input from anthropologists would be useful in this and similar areas.

Simulation models are also underspecified in that linkages between variables are not properly understood. I see the anthropologist entering here both as researcher—to specify and collect the kinds of data needed for better models—and as advisor and evaluator to provide a kind of intellectual caution about the claims that can be made for simulation models given the present state of knowledge. Anthropologists' traditional distrust of quantifying human behavior makes them suitable watchdogs. Anthropologists also perhaps have an unusually well developed appreciation for complexity in human affairs and for the very unpredictable course that human events are likely to take. This appreciation lends itself to evaluation of models which must of necessity be extremely simplified analogies of reality.

Another problem with the use of computer simulation models, especially by systems analysts, is that those who develop these models often have a great regard for the method itself, believing it to be vastly superior to "intuitive" models, that is, any other kind of model. Forrester, the systems analyst who developed the first world model, believes that when human beings try to think ahead to the consequences of the interactions of several variables in a complex system they are "usually wrong." He says, "Our intuition is unreliable. It is worse than random because it is wrong more often than not when faced with the dynamics of complex systems" (1969). This means that for purposes of predicting change in a complex system simulation models are essential, and when developed they become the best analysis of a problem available. There are obvious problems with such a proposition. In addition, it seems that where anthropologists are concerned, the anthropological perspective which emphasizes that models of human behavior should at some level be grounded in human experience is perhaps a useful corrective for an overemphasis on mere technological capability in predicting change in social systems.

That caution is called for in assessing the claims of those who have developed simulation models may be illustrated by the claims made by the authors of *Limits to Growth* for their "World 3" model. Meadows and associates have categorically stated, for example, that "the limits to growth on this planet will be reached in the next one hundred years" (1972: 142); and "even the most optimistic estimates of the benefits of technology in the model did not prevent the ultimate decline of population and industry or in fact did not in any case postpone the collapse beyond the year 2100" (1972: 145). They rather grandly summarize: "We do not expect our broad conclusions to be substantially altered by further revisions" (1972: 22).

Their model has been criticized on a number of grounds: the "benefits of technology" include no new technologies; the model is overaggregated, not even separating rich from poor countries; there are no adaptive social or political feedback processes incorporated into the model (Cole et al. 1973). However, the most serious problem of the model seems to be the degree to which it is underspecified. The model could conceivably be restructured to meet the problems of overaggregation and others, but the authors of *Limits to Growth* themselves admit that "only about 0.1% of the data on the variables required to construct a satisfactory world model is now available" (Freeman 1973: 8). This is a cause for concern if such models are to receive wide media coverage or if they are to be utilized by policy makers. As the authors of *Models of Doom* (Cole et al. 1973) have shown by rerunning the Limits to Growth model under different conditions, the model can of course produce very different results.[2] Carter (1975) succinctly evaluated present thinking on the use of computer simulation models of large-scale human systems: "Their efficacy on macro-systems, where specification is, by necessity, incomplete, is still very much a matter of debate" (1975: 223). My own position in the debate, as I have indicated, is that the use of such models should proceed with caution. Anthropologists concerned with the issues addressed by such models should be prepared to offer constructive criticism and ideas for the research necessary for the development of better models.

CONCLUSION

In this paper I have argued that computer simulation modeling is a useful technique for anthropologists wishing to study change in both theoretical and applied areas. Emphasis has been on the importance of the prior development of a conceptual model that is theoretically lively and empirically sound, rather than on the hardware and software of computer technology. I have attempted, however, to delineate the ways in which the use of the computer extends the possibilities of theoretical models and aids the anthropologist in pursuing the complex problems of predicting change in human communities.

Powerful as it is, the computer is merely an aid, and the abidingly unpredictable nature of human history will surely continue to afflict efforts at augury. One large computer simulation model of economic development in the Punjab, India (Day and Singh 1977), designed to supply policy makers with specific recommendations for the direction that future changes should take, failed to incorporate the energy crisis and high unemployment, thus rendering it a historical study of a short period of Punjabi economic history rather than the set of comprehensive guidelines it was intended to be.

The Punjabi model is instructive as an example. The energy crisis was foreseen by few: it was the result of an unlikely combination of both long-term and rather precipitate sociopolitical events. Meanwhile, the trend toward high unemployment in poor countries has been a sustained development but was not of widespread concern at the time Day and Singh developed their model. It was therefore not incorporated. In this way both sudden events of the most unpredictable nature and slower trends which are difficult to perceive inhibit the prediction of change. As Day and Singh remarked ruefully, "Some unanticipated problems arose" (1977: 157).

Such problems frustrate prediction with or without computer simulation models. They may appear more devastating, however, when work is directed toward a large-scale model or what is taken to be a "complete" system and which entails the decision to become involved in a complex (and complicated) technology. Perhaps such problems will lead investigators to develop better, more fully specified models in an effort to maximize returns and minimize losses on projects as ambitious as the prediction of sociocultural change.

NOTES

1. Stochastic variation is governed by random processes, and a given state may respond to a given input with any one among a range of outputs. The output that occurs occurs at random, so it is impossible to predict the particular output of a single observation in a system.

2. Cole et al. were concerned with the effects of technological progress, and "advances in economic and socio-political activities." They ran the Limits to Growth model with different values for resource base, pollution, agricultural and capital distribution, and so forth, from those used by Meadows et al. (1972).

REFERENCES

Anderson, James M., 1968. Discussions. In *Man the Hunter*, Richard B. Lee and Irven DeVore, eds. (Chicago: Aldine), pp. 150–55.

Birdsell, Joseph B., 1970. Local Group Composition among the Australian Aborigines: A Critique of the Evidence from Fieldwork Conducted since 1930. *Current Anthropology* 11: 115–42.

Carter, Nicholas, 1975. Population, Environment and Natural Resources: A

Critical Review of Recent Models. In *The Population Debate: Dimensions and Perspectives; Papers of the World Population Conference, 1974.* (Bucharest: World Population Conference), pp. 222–31.

Cole, H. S. D., et al., eds., 1973. *Models of Doom: A Critique of the Limits to Growth* (New York: Universe Books).

Darrouzet, Christopher P., 1976. *Systems Theory Belong Cargo.* (M.A. thesis, University of North Carolina).

Day, Richard H., and Inderjit Singh, 1977. *Economic Development as an Adaptive Process: The Green Revolution in the Indian Punjab* (Cambridge: Cambridge University Press).

Elkin, A. P., 1950. The Complexity of Social Organization in Arnhem Land. *Southwestern Journal of Anthropology* 6: 1–20.

Forrester, Jay, 1969. A Deeper Knowledge of Social Systems. *Technology Review* 71: 21–32.

———, 1971. Counterintuitive Nature of Social Systems. *Technology Review* 73: 53.

Freeman, Christopher, 1973. Malthus with a Computer. In *Models of Doom: A Critique of the Limits to Growth,* H. S. D. Cole et al., eds. (New York: Universe Books), pp. 5–13.

Friedenberg, R. M., 1968. *Pioneering Concepts in Modern Science* (New York: Hafner).

Hammel, Eugene A., and Kenneth W. Wachter, 1975. Primonuptiality and Ultimonuptiality: Their Effects on Stem Family Household Frequencies. Unpublished manuscript.

Hiatt, L. R., 1966. The Lost Horde. *Oceania* 37: 81–92.

Jahoda, Marie, 1973. A Postscript on Social Change. In *Models of Doom: A Critique of the Limits to Growth,* H. S. D. Cole et al., eds. (New York: Universe Books), pp. 209–15.

Johnston, F. E., and M. E. Albers, 1973. Computer Simulation of Demographic Processes. In *Methods and Theories of Anthropological Genetics,* M. H. Crawford and P. L. Workman, eds. (Albuquerque: University of New Mexico Press), pp. 202–14.

Kunstadter, Peter, 1973. Footnotes on Implications of Aggregated Data Used in Population Simulations. In *Computer Simulation in Human Population Studies,* Bennett Dyke and Jean W. MacCluer, eds. (New York: Academic Press), pp. 435–46.

Lee, Richard, and Irven DeVore, 1968. *Man the Hunter* (Chicago: Aldine).

MacCluer, Jean W., 1937. Computer Simulation in Anthropology and Human Genetics. In *Methods and Theories of Anthropological Genetics,* M. H. Crawford and P. L. Workman, eds. (Albuquerque: University of New Mexico Press), pp. 220–34.

MacCluer, Jean W., and Bennett Dyke, eds., 1973. *Computer Simulation in Human Population Studies* (New York: Academic Press).

Martin, John F., 1975. On the Estimation of the Sizes of Local Groups in a Hunting-Gathering Environment. *American Anthropologist* 75: 1448–68.

Meadows, Donnella, et al., 1972. *The Limits to Growth* (New York: Universe Books).

Meggitt, Mervyn, 1962. *Desert People: A Study of the Walbiri: Aborigines of Central Australia* (Sydney: Angus and Robertson).

Nardi, Bonnie A., 1977. *Demographic Aspects of Lineage Exogamy in*

Small Populations: A Microsimulation Model (Ph.D. diss., University of California, Irvine).

Peterson, Nicholas, 1975. Hunter-Gatherer Territoriality: The Perspective from Australia. *American Anthropologist* 77: 53–68.

Radcliffe-Brown, A. R., 1930. The Social Organization of Australian Tribes. *Oceania* 1: 1–63, 206–46.

Service, Elman R., 1962. *Primitive Social Organization: An Evolutionary Perspective* (New York: Random House).

Steward, Julian H., 1936. The Economic and Social Basis of Primitive Bands. In *Essays in Honor of A. L. Kroeber* (Berkeley: University of California Press), pp. 331–50.

————, 1968. Causal Factors and Processes in the Evolution of Prefarming Societies. In *Man the Hunter,* Richard Lee and Irven DeVore, eds. (Chicago: Aldine), pp. 321–34.

Tustin, A., 1968. Feedback. In *Mathematical Thinking in Behavioral Sciences: Readings from Scientific American.* (San Francisco: W. H. Freeman), pp. 68–79.

Turnbull, Colin, 1968. The Importance of Flux in Two Hunting Societies. In *Man the Hunter,* Richard Lee and Irven DeVore, eds. (Chicago: Aldine), pp. 132–37.

Williams, B. J., 1974. *A Model of Band Society. Memoirs of the Society for American Archaeology,* No. 29.

Wobst, M., 1975. *The Demography of Finite Populations and the Origins of the Incest Taboo. Memoirs of the Society for American Archaeology,* No. 30.

Pastoral Values among Vulnerable Peasants: Can the Kipsigis of Kenya Keep the Home Fires Burning?

ROBERT E. DANIELS

The Kipsigis are the largest of the Kalenjin-speaking groups in the Rift Valley Province of Kenya.[1] At the start of the twentieth century the Kipsigis numbered less than a hundred thousand people, organized on a tribal level. Like the other Kalenjin groups, they practiced a mixed economy based on pastoralism and hoe cultivation of finger millet, and they occupied highland slopes adjacent to the more arid grasslands typically associated with East African pastoralists.

Kericho District, which roughly corresponds to traditional Kipsigisland, rises from grasslands of around 5,000 feet elevation with 40 inches of rain annually, to forest zones in the east above 7,000 feet with over 70 inches of annual rainfall. Most of the area is composed of hills or folded ridges of red volcanic loam covered throughout the year with bright green vegetation.

In such a lush environment little transhumance was required in the precolonial era to maintain a significant degree of pastoralism. The majority of the population lived in settled communities of dispersed homesteads in the hills. There they maintained gardens, milk cows, sheep, and goats. Depending on local conditions, some men and boys grazed cattle separately in the lower areas, generally to the west. In most cases the cattle camps were not many miles away from the home communities.

In the last seventy-five years Kipsigisland has undergone a visually dramatic transformation. The countryside is now thick with homesteads, generally of ten to twenty acres each, forming a continuous quilt of enclosed rectilinear fields devoted to several different crops and pasturage. In the most "developed" areas rectangular houses with corrugated aluminum roofs are common, the hillsides are contour plowed by tractors, and indigenous trees such as the flat topped acacias have been replaced with tall, straight, imported species, thus creating landscapes more suggestive of Europe than Africa. In the northern part of the district, adjacent to Kericho town, tea estates cover the hills for miles. Many commercial trucks and government vehicles pass along the main road every hour of the day, scores of buses run regular routes between the town of Kericho and the many smaller trading centers, and bicycles are familiar throughout the countryside.

Almost everyone has abandoned most traditional dress and ornaments. In the more remote areas a middle-aged man might wear khaki shorts, a simple shirt, sandals, and perhaps a blanket, while a farm wife typically wears a plain cotton dress, a headscarf, and a shawl or baby-wrapper. Everywhere, however, younger people aspire to the styles of the towns. Where forty years ago young men wore their hair in greased and ochred braids, kept their ears stretched and laden with beads, wore cloaks over their shoulders, and carried spears in their hands, many now wear leather shoes, long trousers, nylon shirts and neckties, suit jackets or acrylic sweaters, and occasionally carry transistor radios. The Kipsigis, described on the dust jacket of Peristiany's monograph published in 1939 as "one of the most handsome and warlike Kenya highland tribes" now give the appearance of a relatively prosperous peasantry.

What are the processes underlying these changes, and what do they imply for the future?

THE MODEL

I will attempt to answer these questions using the cybernetic mode of analysis pioneered by Bateson (1972). Adaptation can be defined as the process by which a self-organizing system maintains continuity and balance in both its internal organization and its relationship to its environment in the face of change. In any system there are certain variables whose values must be maintained within relatively narrow limits if the system is to persist. In Ashby's model (1956) these are called the system's *essential variables*. Adaptation is accomplished most efficiently if negative feedback regulates the system's more peripheral and more flexible (nonessential) variables in ways which counteract environmental disturbances before they can reach the essential variables. For example, skin temperature in a mammal must be varied frequently in order to maintain blood temperature within the range of viability. Natural systems contain a large number of levels arranged in a "defense in depth" (Bateson 1972: 351) so that they tend to respond first on the level which promises, from past experience, to suffice most quickly, with the least energy expenditure, and with the least constraint (Miller 1965; Rappaport 1974).

In this paper I will use an organic analogy between adaptation in ecosystems and cultural systems suggested by Ramón Margalef (1968). The basic premise of this model is that, if exogenous factors are stable for a long period, a living system will tend to evolve toward greater efficiency in the conversion of energy into structure, or encoded information. In Margalef's terms, the system increases in *maturity*. More energy is captured and greater use is made of available energy as it flows throughout the system. As matter and energy are added, the informational capacity of the system is multiplied; the specialization and diversity of components increases, and that amounts to an increasingly detailed mapping of, or more finely tuned adaptation to, the context. Certainty within the system increases. The changes experienced by component parts of the system shift from direct reactions to external disturbances, to rhythmic responses to signals filtered through other parts of the system. Fluctuations in the populations of component species are dampened and there is a relative constancy of numbers. Increased internal regulation through interaction (negative feedback) diminishes the chance of outbreaks (positive feedback processes which have overwhelmed local regulation). Reproductive strategies shift from quantity to quality. In general, as maturity increases, member species become increasingly interdependent.

Margalef's second basic point is that "any exchange between two systems of different information content does not result in a partition or equalization of the information, but increases the difference" (1968: 16). He goes on to state, even more directly, "A more mature system always exploits a less mature system" (1968: 37).

Let us, for simplicity, label the more mature system A and the less mature B. Just as "the process of self-organization [within a single system] stops when fluctuations are unpredictable or insurmountable" (1968: 33), these new exchanges between systems tend to halt the trend toward maturity and endogenous synchronization in the subordinate subsystem, B. System A interferes in B's internal processes according to criteria that are initially, in terms of B's organization, arbitrary. Those components in B which are most complexly dependent upon other parts of the subsystem are most vulnerable in the new contact situation. In ecosystems, for example, the species most likely to suffer are those with "the most advanced examples of defense—mimicry, animal poisons, elaborate symbiotic relations, and complicated territorial behavior" (1968: 91). With the loss of the more exotic middlemen, the relationships between remaining components are interrupted or become short-circuited. Noise increases.

In contrast, system A's actions reward those components of B which can most quickly expand to make use of the new inputs, that is, species with the shortest life-span, highest metabolisms, and greatest reproductive potential—species variously described as "pioneer," "prodigal," or "opportunistic" (1968: 88). Hence B's regulators in the most flexible circuits become incorporated into larger circuits in which they have lost control to components in A. A thus not only short-circuits the most particularized aspects of B, it also coopts, or 'long-circuits,' the most generalized aspects of B. To the extent that B retains limited autonomy as a subsystem, it attempts to protect its own essential variables, whether or not they receive A's direct attention, as best it can.

The exchange between the two systems goes both ways, of course. The extent to which B's excess production is pumped into A is a measure of the degree of exploitation in the situation. Without exploitation maturity would spread from A to B and they would become less and less distinct as subsystems. Strong exploitation keeps B in a "steady state of low maturity" (1968: 38). Where exploitation occurs "it is advantageous for the more mature and exploiting system to develop sinuosities and stretch the length of the boundary to the maximum . . . in the less mature communities the trend must be to reduce to the minimum the extension of the boundaries that are potential sites of exploitation" (1968: 41).

While Margalef's model is based on examples far removed from our immediate interests (his own research is with plankton), it is a highly suggestive analogue of the theory of dependency and underdevelopment. The utility of the model is hampered, however, by its generality. Culture contact situations vary widely. I have therefore been seeking further ideas in the life sciences which may more closely resemble certain features of the situation among the Kipsigis. I will briefly mention two.

The cybernetic model of adaptation can too easily be mistaken for a Panglossian view that all is for the best and that evil does not really exist. We are all aware, however, that culture contact situations frequently contain pathogenic contradictions. Bateson's analysis of alcoholism (1972: 309–37) suggests a dynamic tangle that may be analogous to the situation at hand. Many of the material and symbolic items introduced into the Kipsigis system resemble addictive substances. I will return to this point at the end of the paper.

Another line of thought deals with domestication. I view domestication as one of a variety of specific processes subsumed by Margalef's general model, and one which, by analogy, describes many of the characteristics of the adaptation of the Kipsigis sociocultural system to colonial rule and the cash economy.

HISTORY

Destabilization and Pacification. It is perhaps two hundred years since the Kipsigis entered their present area from the northeast. During the nineteenth century the Kipsigis expanded southward against the Masai and westward against the Gusii and Luo, securing a large and coherent land base.[2]

Late in the nineteenth century infections preceded the arrival of significant numbers of Europeans.[3] During the 1880s a rinderpest epidemic swept through East Africa killing a majority of the cattle. The sharp reduction in cattle lead to a great intensification in warfare. On one major raid into Masailand the warriors contracted smallpox. On their return they infected others, causing a great many deaths.[4] Further destabilization during this period is exemplified by the Battle of Mogori. A few years before Pax Britannica the southern Kipsigis suffered a major military defeat by Gusii and Luo forces, combined in an unprecedented alliance.

In evaluating the protohistorical period it is important to dispel the notion that the British found a static, tradition-bound society. The Kipsigis had had a dynamic relationship with their various neighbors and, at the time of pacification, their system was in an unusually fluid state. In particular, the many setbacks of the years immediately preceding and the resulting underutilization of much of the land in what became Kericho District must have heightened the expansionist tendencies of the Kipsigis. Their system was dynamically vulnerable to forces promoting immaturity.

Significant British presence came with the construction of the Kenya-Uganda railroad. From 1895 to 1906 the neighboring, and closely related, Nandi fought a series of bloody campaigns against the intruders. Through skillful diplomacy the British managed to keep most of the Kipsigis out of the Nandi wars and established a post at Kericho in 1903. Punitive expeditions were organized, however, against the southern Kipsigis in 1905 and again in 1912 to suppress Kipsigis encroachment against the Masai and Gusii. In both cases the Kipsigis forces were dispersed with few casualties and large numbers of stock were seized (Moyse-Bartlett 1956: 208). From time to time during the ensuing decades colonial troops were called out to restore order along the tribal borders, but the Kipsigis never engaged in a direct rebellion against the colonial power. In fact, the Kipsigis willingly cooperated with the British in the mid 1930s in the identification of sorcerers *(orgoiik)* who were rounded up and removed from the district.

These events, I suggest, are analogous to the first steps in domestication, in which the potential domesticate is constrained from interacting with its natural context, is exposed to strong efforts to diminish or remove its capacity for defense, and finds itself dependent upon the domesticator for protection from internal and external dangers (defined as much by the domesticator as by the domesticate) and vulnerable to the threat of force by its new protector. If this can be achieved without destroying the subordinate system's processes of self-maintenance, the dominant system is then in a position to promote or suppress specific features in the other. With this in mind, let us briefly consider the policies of the early colonial period.

Colonial "Development." Early British policy was aimed at the "depastoralisation" of the Kipsigis and their conversion into a supporting role in the colonial economy. By 1903 Asian traders had already branched out into the countryside trading metal tools, wire, beads, cloth, salt, sugar, and other goods for millet flour and cowhides. Starting with rather limited barter, their trade in subsequent years became a major inducement for Kipsigis to become involved in the cash economy. Missionaries were supported by the administration in the hope that they would replace indigenous rituals and beliefs—in Rappaport's terms (1971) the higher order regulators of a society—with those more conducive to civilization. In the words of the first missionary to the Kipsigis, "Every pagan brought to Christ becomes in the very nature of the case an asset in the economic structure instead of a liability" (quoted in Manners 1967: 347).

The collection of hut tax began in 1904. At first taxes were payable in kind, but the administration soon pressed for payments in cash. The real importance of taxation lay not in generating revenue but in initiating the diversion of native efforts into the wider economy dominated by European interests (cf. Mitchell 1970; Watson 1970).

Starting in 1906, British settlers obtained large tracts of land along the railway and around Kericho. Further land was alienated to the southwest, ostensibly to form a buffer between the Kipsigis and the Gusii. During the colonial period the settlers' farms produced milk, beef, maize, and a variety of other cash crops. Thousands of Kipsigis came to be employed on these estates. As was typical of much colonial employment, wages did not constitute a true subsistence income but amounted to a cash supplement to whatever the workers could derive from their homes in the reserve or produce on their own using estate land. A frequent arrangement granted the resident workers, or "squatters," the use of grazing land (from which they or their tribesmen had previously been evicted) in exchange for training and using their oxen to plow the settler's fields. Many Kipsigis learned maize cultivation in this way. The administration soon pressured them to adopt maize in the reserve.

World War I drew large numbers of men into wage labor and into the auxiliary forces in the campaign against the Germans in Tanganyika.[5] Further destabilization of the reserve population by influenza and crop failures (Wrigley 1965: 233) was followed by the postwar boom in agricultural exports from European farms. Tea, first planted near Kericho in 1912, became a major plantation crop after the first processing factory was opened in 1924 (Manners 1967: 310). Although the Kipsigis never constituted more than a minority of the work force on the tea estates, wage labor on European farms rose dramatically as European settlement was increased by Soldier Settler Schemes.[6] The problem throughout Kenya Colony, however, was how to induce a greater proportion of local labor away from the more efficient small holdings in the reserves. The solution was to raise taxes and depress wages.

Meanwhile the first plow to be owned by Kipsigis was used in the reserve in 1921, an innovation that many soon copied (Manners 1967: 288). Maize thus became a more productive, though less nutritious, alternative to the traditional staple food, eleusine millet, which required fresh land with each planting and a great deal of hand labor. Colonial policy granted white settlers monopoly rights over the major cash crops (tea, coffee, European strains of dairy cattle) while promoting increased production of maize by the Kipsigis as a source of food for the growing plantation work force. As the colonial government hoped, more land came under maize to meet these increased markets and to provide cash for the increasing number of trade goods (maintained at relatively high prices by tariff regulations). Another cause for increased maize cultivation, less directly a concern of the administration, was to support the rapidly growing population in the reserve. As Colin Leys (1975) has argued, the profitability achieved by the private European mixed farms was made possible only by the legally engineered underdevelopment of the reserves.

In adapting to these changes, the Kipsigis system had incorporated processes which had dynamic implications beyond those intended by the British. A major example of this is the spread of land enclosure. Manners (1967: 292) traces the start of land enclosure to a mission-trained Kipsigis farmer involved in cash-cropping maize. In 1930 this man plowed a field too large to be fenced in the manner of a traditional patch of millet. Soon embroiled with his neighbors over incursions by their animals, he persuaded them to plant their millet gardens around his field, with each man fencing his share of the outside perimeter. Since millet plots are not replanted a second year, he then expanded his maize to the fence. A few years later he completed the inversion of traditional spatial order by placing his cattle *inside* the fence. As Manners comments, "The process of land accumulation by this man was only stopped when his neighbors undertook the cultivation of maize and defended themselves against further encroachment by this means and by the erection of paddock fences" (1967: 292).

And so, while the British pondered over land policy (see, for example, Orchardson 1935), enclosure spread in a self-reinforcing manner. Twenty years after enclosure started, virtually all usable land was divided and individually claimed. Enclosure produced many hundreds of court cases, and although many were relatively minor squabbles among neighbors, a certain amount of injustice also occurred (Manners 1967: 296). As Margalef's model would predict, some of the men appointed by the government as chiefs and subchiefs were among the more prominent opportunists. Still, the most remarkable feature of enclosure was that it was compatible with the preexisting settlement pattern of dispersed homesteads and caused so little immediate change.

Most of the visually striking changes appeared during World War II and the postwar period. A large proportion of Kipsigis men entered the army and served in North Africa and the Far East. This period also saw expansion of the tea estates, prosperity among white settlers, and a major increase in the impact of the colonial government through road building, a system of native courts, and so on. Schools, originally introduced with coercive pressure, became available to a significant minority and were sought after by the many. School fees became established as a major cash demand on most Kipsigis families. The rudiments of modern medicine were sufficiently available to have been used by the vast majority of families, at least in times of crisis.

In both education and medicine, the key impetus was supplied by missionaries working in cooperation with the government. Their effectiveness on a purely religious level has been far less. While today almost everyone declares himself to be Christian, missionary teachings have not been deeply absorbed or syncretically woven into daily life.[7]

Virtually everyone, however, became involved to some degree with the cash economy. In 1959 the value of sales through the Maize Marketing Board exceeded $200,000 even though the majority of maize in excess of domestic needs was being sold privately to tea estate workers,

to Masai and Luo in border markets, and on the black market to Kipsigis middlemen (Manners 1967: 301). During the same year regulated
sales of cattle and cattle products approached $300,000.

The Modern Era. Economic intensification increased still further in
the last years of the colonial regime and has continued at an accelerat-
ing rate after independence. In 1957 the first Kipsigis small holdings in
tea were planted. Today thousands of homesteads are involved. In 1959
the tea estates ceased supplying workers with maize rations purchased
from European settlers; thus Kipsigis small-scale cash-crop farmers
gained access to an enormous new market. In 1960 the ban against
African ownership of European "grade" cattle was lifted, allowing development of commercial milk production that had already started with
native cattle and grade cattle owned surreptitiously.

Political events outside the district brought the era of the white settlers in Kenya to a close. Government schemes, starting in 1961 and
continuing after independence, purchased European estates and sub-
divided them, at calculated densities, among African small holders. By
1968 a few European settlers remained in the northern end of the district, and the tea estates were still expanding, but the majority of the
formerly alienated land was being resettled by Kipsigis under government direction. The new homesteaders assumed ten-year development
loans and thirty-year mortgages at commercial rates and were required
to start modern farming with grade cattle, tractors, hybrid maize, super-
phosphate fertilizers, and, where applicable, tea. While most people on
the schemes found themselves squeezed between government suppliers
and government buyers,[8] many of these same changes were being volun-
tarily adopted in the former reserve at the same time, apparently with
some success. During the 1960s the black market price for maize was
more than double the official rate and government control was not effective in most areas outside the schemes.

By the early 1970s business was booming. All major indicators of the
commercialization of the countryside were increasing rapidly. A few
individuals started to accumulate land holdings totalling over a hundred
acres in the former reserve, while a large proportion of the people faced
the prospect of having to subdivide family plots into smaller units than
ever before.

Population and Land. Population had increased rapidly during the
colonial era. In 1939 Peristiany (1939: 1) estimated a Kipsigis population of 80,000. The 1948 census figure was 157,211. The 1962 census
figure was 341,711 Kipsigis, of whom 84 percent were in Kericho District. Most of those absent were men between 20 and 35 years old (Morgan and Shaffer 1966; Ominde 1968: 176). The 1969 census counted

471,459 Kipsigis; extrapolation from these census data suggests that the Kipsigis now number over 600,000. The age-sex pyramid shows the classic pattern of an immature population (Margalef 1968: 90), with a broad base representing an overburden of dependents due to a high birth rate, and sharply narrowing sides indicating a significant rate of death at all ages. At present the median age is around 15 or 16 years.

Many of the effects of population growth have been slow to emerge, however, because of the extensive land base with which the Kipsigis started the colonial era. At the start of the century only one fifth of the total area controlled was being used for settled communities, with a density of 150 to 200 persons per square mile (Pilgrim 1961: 33). Now the whole district has been homesteaded and enclosed. The 1962 census indicated an average density of 264 per square mile in the former reserve. While the density varies with the fertility of the soil, even the densest areas are still, by Kenyan standards, uncrowded, and the Kipsigis have been able to maintain conditions similar to those for which their domestic institutions are adapted. Thus much of the impact of the population explosion on family and community organization has been delayed for one or two generations. There is no doubt, however, that population pressure now threatens to overload both traditional and modern institutions.

ESSENTIAL VARIABLES

East African pastoralists are well known for their stubborn devotion to the "cattle-complex" and their lack of interest in modernization. Considering their rapid development, the Kipsigis *appear* to be a clear counter-example. Manners states that "most of [the Kipsigis] seem eager to discard the old for this new [world]" (1968: 222). In my experience this statement, if taken as a description of individual orientation, applies to only a small majority of the population. On the societal level Manners's statement contains a questionable assumption about economic and social dynamics: the relationship between cash-crop agriculture and wage employment on the one hand and pastoralism on the other is far more complex than the unilineal replacement process Manners suggests.

My own fieldwork focused on a grasslands community on the edge of the more fertile hills. Although primarily a grazing area in the past and not now noted for progress, all homesteads in the area are involved in some cash-cropping. After my lengthy discussion of change it may come as a small surprise to learn that the Kipsigis still keep large numbers of native cattle. Homestead herds ranged from 13 to 32 head, or 2.6 cattle per person, a figure that compares favorably with such confirmed pastoralists as the Nuer, the Dodoth, and the Pakot.[8]

Along with the cattle themselves, the Kipsigis have maintained the set of social principles premised on cattle that characterizes East African pastoralism (Daniels 1975). Most significantly, the kinship system seems little changed from precolonial days; descent and marriage continue to be defined in terms of rights to cattle. Bridewealth continues to be paid in cattle, though now augmented with cash and trade goods. Paternity is defined contractually by bridewealth, a large proportion of marriages are still arranged, leviratic marriage of widows is the norm, and one of the hallmarks of East African pastoralism, marriage between an old woman who lacks sons and a young bride, still occurs regularly. Compensation for homicide, intentional and accidental, continues to be paid in cattle, and quite apart from any court action, cattle are still being seized by force in cases of homicide and elopement. Polygyny continues to be very common. In a sample taken in 1967, 208 men aged 20 to 75 were married to 329 women; 39 percent of the men were polygynous, and the majority—61 percent—of the women had cowives.

Male initiation, although now restricted by law to the six-week school vacation, is still universal. The symbolism of initiation is still heavily pastoral, as are the virtues it stresses. While a small number of highly educated females have successfully avoided initiation, most school girls and all girls not in school are initiated; the latter are secluded, as in the past, for a number of months.

The retention of so many aspects of the pastoralist system cannot be dismissed as the last fragments of an incomplete acculturation. Clearly a more dynamic interpretation is necessary. From a viewpoint that stresses the initiative of the larger system, one can say that the fertility of Kericho District has permitted Kipsigis society to be bloated into a state of highly productive immaturity, i.e., domestication. In terms of the adaptive initiative of the smaller system, I argue that the abundance of land, and those proceeds of its fertility which have remained within the smaller system, have been used to subsidize the essential social and psychological variables of pastoralism. The persistence of this core of traditions is not immediately obvious to the non-Kipsigis, for the cultural forms have been stripped of their more dramatic and exotic expressions and are embedded in the "down-home" ordinary events of familial and dyadic relationships. Taken together, the features mentioned here combine to produce a vast social network which, being uncentralized, is not readily comprehended until one pieces together a great deal of private information.

The social network is continually renewed as all but one of an elder's mature sons establish separate homesteads, usually in other communities, while daughters are married to nearby families. Thus communities are neither bounded descent groups nor loose collections of neighbors who happen to interact on a daily basis, but particularly dense clusters of relationships, the majority of which are *affinal,* woven into a seamless social fabric that extends throughout the district. There are in addition several modes of relationship beyond kinship (for example, women's cooperative work sets and bonds between men initiated together). Inasmuch as descent and affinity mean sharing and exchanging livestock, family herds are similarly intertwined. Cattle are further redistributed by a system of private partnerships *(kimanagan)* which is very widespread, if not universal. Neighbors are those who share fire from hearth to hearth. In this practical act the Kipsigis see a rich metaphor of their society.

In such a network behavior is governed by the multiple relationships which impinge on any individual decision. On the societal level the very high degree of redundancy ensures stability of norms and values. The patterns of what people do and what they agree should be done are little affected by individual shortcomings and idiosyncracies. It is this informational resilience, anchored in cattle, that the Kipsigis have defended through seventy-five years of change.

THE FUTURE

One of the fundamental premises that has shaped the evolution of Kipsigis culture is that the only way to create a cow is with another cow. Deeply encoded in the core institutions is the message that continuity of herd and family is a sine qua non. In situations of microadaptation no man has the right to make decisions for another, but on any issue involving the maintenance of basic patterns, consensus and cooperation must override individual choice. At present, however, there are many situations in which it is not clear what the long-range implications of individual actions will be, for they become caught up in new circuits and amplified in new ways.

In trying to second-guess the future I will first focus on the immediate continuities and the trends for change that have become well established within Kipsigis society through interaction with the larger system. Finally, I will briefly speculate on the implications of trends in the larger system.

Local Trends. As long as the Kipsigis are able to avoid abrupt change in their domestic social processes, particularly in the network of marriage ties based on exchanges of rights in cattle, the future appears to be fairly predictable. The shared sense of order which this system gives to individual lives makes it highly unlikely that there will be widespread changes in individual thinking on deeper epistemological levels. I do not expect any rapid increase in the penetration of missionary teachings into most lives. I doubt the possibility that the initiation ceremonies, for all the lack of correspondence that has developed between their manifest content and their present social context, will be replaced by operations at medical clinics and marked by minor Christian observances, as has happened in some Bantu groups.

For similar reasons, I do not expect the Kipsigis to mount any modern political action. As long as people define themselves in terms of the uncentralized web of relationships, I do not see them mobilizing in large numbers behind any institutionalized authority. A prepolitical movement of Kipsigis against Kipsigis is out of the question, and since the political situation in Kenya rules against the efficacy of both traditional ad hoc mobilizations against non-Kipsigis and modern political agitation, I do not predict any major redefinition of the boundary which separates the Kipsigis from those who control the institutions of modernization. Thus one can expect a continuation of the current relationship between the Kipsigis system and the larger economy.

Undoubtedly involvement in wage labor will increase a great deal, but here the Kipsigis will find themselves competing for unskilled jobs against the growing number of landless, and hence economically more desperate, people from other areas, while most of the better paying jobs have already been preempted—in many cases whole economic niches are already dominated by single ethnic groups.

At home the traditional mode of social organization has been highly successful in extending itself, at every opportunity, through homesteading new land. Yet the family network has not taken root in urban areas. Wage labor, it appears, will continue to be used in an attempt to maintain the status quo back home.

The economic squeeze will undoubtedly intensify. In the long run grade cattle may totally replace native cattle in the fertile hills, as has happened in other areas of Kenya. Obviously, this would have serious effects on social organization. I am not convinced, however, that all native cattle will disappear from the system in the foreseeable future. I find it hard to believe that grade cattle will compete successfully with native cattle in the lower zones. I also note that the system of cattle partnerships persists and that many people in the hills and most, perhaps all, of the people resettled on the schemes (where native cattle are prohibited) keep native livestock with friends in the lower areas. I thus predict that a large sector of the population will be able to maintain the currency of traditionally defined marriage.

The individual Kipsigis, caught between rising economic demands and a shrinking land base, finds (whatever his personal motivations) that the solution almost always involves further contact with the wider system and thus more exposure to its negative effects. However, the options for increasing agricultural production (maize, tea, and coffee) are more responsive to capital intensification than to labor intensification.

The population problem may well be the undoing of the egalitarianism implicit in traditional organization. The inversion of spatial definitions is beginning to invert the logic of family organization, especially polygyny and the associated house-property complex. Once a man with two wives had two farms. Today he is likely to have two half-farms. To persist with polygyny threatens to impoverish the family. One can therefore expect polygyny to decline sharply as population pressures become critical. A reduction in polygyny will reinforce the effects of the cash economy in leading to a differentiation in the accumulation of capital and a loss of the mutual interdependence which marked tribal organization.

Recently the national government has instituted a program to survey and register all land holdings. While proceeding, at least at first, only in those communities in which individual claims are not in dispute, the program has not met with enthusiasm. At the time of my research most people saw little benefit in accepting a new set of fees and expenses, giving government courts a say in future land transfers (now private and familial affairs), or in creating accurate records which would threaten their "catch me if you can" approach to paying taxes. Whatever its intent, land registration promises to become an official sanction for the accumulation of large and multiple holdings by the more successful modern farmers. The issues involved in land registration clearly exemplify Margalef's point that subsystem A will seek to maximize, and subsystem B to minimize, their points of informational contact.

I believe that a consideration of several other features of traditional family organization and marriage networks would reveal similar dynamic inversions in which, at some critical level of population density, the former strengths of the system become major liabilities. Over time the various economic changes threaten to simplify, weaken, or render irrelevant existing shared meanings. Individualization increases the vulnerability of the Kipsigis to further exploitation. Although I do not think social cohesion will be undone all at once, the projection of present trends, if allowed to continue long enough, will bring about the loss of much information currently encoded in social structure and result in a shift from a society based on shared fate to a society rapidly differentiating into the haves and the have-nots.

The Kipsigis and Larger Trends. Having come to this rather unhappy prospect, I think there are three reasons for returning once again to Margalef's model.

First, I have left implicit, as he does, the question of defining the immaturity of the system relative to its scale. The system which has intruded upon the Kipsigis, however one defines its boundaries, has a very high level of maturity. Yet in Margalef's terms there are many features of the world system which seem to be increasing in immaturity, for example, the loss of linguistic diversity with the spread of major languages, or the replacement of mixed farming with agribusiness.

Second, as I indicated earlier, the changes that have occurred among the Kipsigis have frequently taken the form of an addiction. Many of the actions and substances which were adopted in order to preserve the autonomy of the local system in the colonial context (for example, maize cultivation and wage labor) have produced paradoxical effects, since they are adaptive in the short run while generating long-term positive feedback processes which amplify the original predicament. In Kenya, as in the United States, the solution to problems arising out of rapid growth is too often seen as a little more growth. It is useful to consider what has fostered these contradictions introduced into the Kipsigis system.

Third, Margalef's model begs the question of what might happen should a sudden change occur in the context of the *larger* system. Clearly the predictions based on what "more of the same" would do to the Kipsigis must be altered if there is reason to believe that "more of the same" will not be forthcoming.

All three considerations—the growing immaturity, the addictive aspects, and the instability of the world system—can be traced, as Margalef's model suggests, to enormous increases in free energy, in this case fossil fuels. The relevance of this is immediate when one reflects that the current interchange between the Kipsigis and the national and international economy is now largely predicated on petroleum.

There are many predictions concerning the oil supply; perhaps it is sufficient here to note the conclusions of the Workshop on Alternate Energy Strategies (Flower 1978). They estimate that, on a worldwide basis, production will fail to meet demand sometime before the year 2000—indeed, considering probable OPEC policies, sometime in the 1980s. As the turning point draws nearer I think we can expect to see an increase in last-minute exploitation of rich environments such as the East African highlands. Perhaps this is what I have been describing.

A failure of oil production to keep up with demand must surely lead to higher prices and economic recession, particularly in a country like Kenya that generates a major portion of its foreign exchange from tourism and relies heavily on road transport. It seems likely that areas in the periphery of the world system will experience the withdrawal of fuels more sharply than the core.

If all this is true, then the timing of these events becomes critical for the Kipsigis. Judging from the experience of other highland groups, I would predict that the Kipsigis can sustain the current rate of growth in population for another generation with some serious problems but without a general collapse. The sooner economic development in its current form peaks out, the more leeway the Kipsigis will have to adjust to the situation using the large measure of social and economic autonomy they have been able to conserve. In the words of Howard Odum, "In times of declining energy quantity and quality, the economics of scale shifts to smaller dispersed units" (1976: 269). The Kipsigis are still largely preadapted to a coming age of low energy. To quote a Kipsigis saying, "In the afternoon the shade is on the other side of the tree."

When all this occurs, if it does, the Kipsigis will still face the enormous problem of regaining control over population expansion. Changes in this direction so far are very modest, and the traditional family patterns, on which so much depends, also continue to promote large families for several mutually reinforcing reasons. I am at a loss to predict how the demographic transition will come about. I can only conclude that if circumstances shift control of such problems back to the local level fairly soon, the Kipsigis may still reach a new homeostasis based on the accumulated wisdom encoded in their culture, which has served them so well this far.

NOTES

1. Fieldwork among the Kipsigis was conducted from August 1965 to March 1968 and again in June 1972. It was supported by a grant from the National Science Foundation and through research appointments to the Cross-Cultural Study of Ethnocentrism Project and the Child Development Research Unit (University of Nairobi), both funded by the Carnegie Corporation of New York. I am also indebted to the University Research Council of the University of North Carolina for making possible the very able assistance I have received from R. Bruce Clymer in the development of the ideas presented in this paper.

2. Many Kipsigis descent groups *(ortinwek)* are said to be derived from Nandi, Okiek, Masai, and Gusii immigrants and captives. In particular, several descent groups which are heavily represented in the southern portion of the district trace their derivation to Gusii lineages which were surrounded and absorbed en masse as the Kipsigis expanded.

3. Although protohistorical evidence is meager, it does not appear that nineteenth-century Arab slave caravans had much contact with the Kipsigis. Between 1886 and 1896 half a dozen British and German expeditions reached Kipsigisland. One of them became involved in a major skirmish, but the others seem to have passed without incident (Manners 1967: 223).

4. On this raid the younger warriors killed and mutilated Masai women in order to plunder brass coils from their arms and legs. Brass was a trade good that had not yet appeared in Kipsigisland. The events also indicate the desperate lack of livestock at home with which to support dependents; bridewealth averaged eight to ten head of cattle, and under normal conditions these women would have been adopted as wives and daughters. The Kipsigis interpret the smallpox epidemic as divine retribution for these atrocities.

5. "Some 47,000 Africans from East Africa died on war service" (Middleton 1965: 353).

6. Begun in 1919, the Soldier Settler Schemes were a device used by settlers to increase their numbers by making large areas in Kericho, Nandi, and other districts available to British veterans, particularly former officers, at very low cost (Bennett 1965: 233, 241).

7. Many of the early converts to the Protestant missions left the church over the issues of polygyny and of native beer. A small number of men who were circumcised by mission personnel later paid high fees to have their status endorsed by attending traditional rites, after they became the targets of severe social pressure. Informants also claimed that some women, who had been convinced by missionaries in the early years to forego initiation, later underwent the ceremony in order to be able to attend their daughters' initiations. Kipsigis informants claim, and my impressions agree (although I do not have systematic information about this), that those communities most affected by mission teachings have higher rates of social and psychological disorder (broken homes, illegitimacy, and so forth). In cybernetic terms, this would be called *noise*.

8. See Leys (1975) for a discussion of the British and World Bank loans underwriting the resettlement schemes, and the national and international renegotiations which became necessary when a majority of the small farmers on the early schemes failed to keep up with loan repayments. On a more personal level one of the hundreds of 45 rpm records recorded by Kipsigis musicians in Kericho during the 1960s starts with the spoken words "song of the scheme" and contains the following line comparing Kenyatta's imprisonment during the Emergency with the new mortgages: "Kenyatta was tied up for seven years; we, the people of the scheme, have been tied up for thirty." Sung in Kipsigis, and labelled *"Bane Rogoroni?"* (Does This Beer Tube Bewitch?"), the record apparently escaped the notice of the national government.

9. In comparison, Evans-Pritchard's estimate for the Nuer, whose herds were still depleted by rinderpest, was less than 1.5 cattle per person (1940:

20). Thomas (1965: 22) gives figures suggesting about 3.5 cattle per person for a Dodoth neighborhood. 1952 government figures for the Pakot, who are an example of "pastoral resistance to change" (Schneider 1959), work out to "an average of 10 to 20 head of cattle per adult man in the main pastoral areas and an average of from 2 to 5 head in the more heavily agricultural areas" (Schneider 1957: 279). The numbers for the Kipsigis community I studied, in the more pastoral part of Kericho District, are 17.4 cattle per married man (including dependent sons, or 22 per homestead). I do not have figures for the Kipsigis highland areas, but they are certainly higher than those cited for the Pakot (Daniels 1975).

REFERENCES

Ashby, W. Ross, 1956. *An Introduction to Cybernetics* (London: Chapman and Hall).

Bateson, Gregory, 1972. *Steps to an Ecology of Mind* (New York: Ballentine Books).

Bennett, George, 1965. Settlers and Politics in Kenya, up to 1945. In *The History of East Africa, Volume 2*, V. Harlow and E. M. Chilver, eds. (London: Oxford University Press), pp. 265–332.

Daniels, Robert E., 1975. Pastoralists with Plows: Cultural Continuities among the Kipsigis of Kenya. Paper presented at the 74th Annual Meeting of the American Anthropological Association, San Francisco.

Evans-Pritchard, E. E., 1940. *The Nuer* (London: Oxford University Press).

Flower, Andrew R., 1978. World Oil Production. *Scientific American* 238: 42–49.

Leys, Colin, 1975. *Underdevelopment in Kenya: The Political Economy of Neo-Colonialism 1964–1971* (Berkeley: University of California Press).

Manners, Robert A., 1967. The Kipsigis of Kenya: Culture Change in a "Model" East African Tribe. In *Contemporary Change in Traditional Societies: Volume 1, Introduction and African Tribes*, J. H. Steward, ed. (Urbana: University of Illinois Press), pp. 205–359.

Margalef, Ramón, 1968. *Perspectives in Ecological Theory* (Chicago: University of Chicago Press).

Middleton, J., 1965. Kenya: Changes in African Life, 1912–1945. In *The History of East Africa, Volume 2*, V. Harlow and E. M. Chilver, eds. (London: Oxford University Press), pp. 333–94.

Miller, James G., 1965. Living Systems: Cross-Level Hypotheses. *Behavioral Science* 10: 380–411.

Mitchell, J. Clyde, 1970. The Causes of Labor Migration. In *Black Africa*, John Middleton, ed. (New York: Macmillan), pp. 23–37.

Morgan, W.T.W. and N. Manfred Shaffer, 1966. *Population of Kenya: Density and Distribution* (Nairobi: Oxford University Press).

Moyse-Bartlett, H., 1956. *The King's African Rifles* (Aldershot, England: Gale and Polden).

Odum, Howard T., 1976. Net Energy Analysis of Alternatives for the United States. Hearings before the Subcommittee on Energy and Power of the

Committee on Interstate and Foreign Commerce, House of Representatives. *Congressional Record* Serial No. 94–63: 253–302.

Ominde, S. H., 1968. *Land and Population Movements in Kenya* (Evanston, Ill.: Northwestern University Press).

Orchardson, Ian Q., 1935. Future Development of the Kipsigis with Special Reference to Land Tenure. *The Journal of the East Africa and Uganda Natural History Society* 12: 200–210.

Peristiany, J. G., 1939. *The Social Institutions of the Kipsigis* (London: George Routledge and Sons).

Pilgrim, J. W., 1961. The Social and Economic Consequences of Land Enclosure in the Kipsigis Reserve. Unpublished manuscript (Kampala: East African Institute for Social Research).

Rappaport, Roy A., 1971. Ritual, Sanctity, and Cybernetics. *American Anthropologist* 73: 59–76.

———, 1974. Maladaptation in Social Systems. Paper presented in the Carolina Population Center Lecture/Discussion Series, Feb. 10, 1975, Chapel Hill, N.C.

Schneider, Harold K., 1957. The Subsistence Role of Cattle among the Pakot and in East Africa. *American Anthropologist* 59: 278–300.

———, 1959. Pakot Resistance to Change. In *Continuity and Change in African Cultures*, W. R. Bascom and M. J. Herskovits, eds. (Chicago: University of Chicago Press), pp. 144–67.

Thomas, Elizabeth M., 1965. *Warrior Herdsmen* (New York: Vintage Books).

Watson, William, 1970. Migrant Labor and Detribalization. In *Black Africa*, John Middleton, ed. (New York: Macmillan), pp. 38–48.

Wrigley, C. C., 1965. Kenya: The Patterns of Economic Life: 1902–1945. In *The History of East Africa, Volume 2*, V. Harlow and E. M. Chilver, eds. (London: Oxford University Press), pp. 209–64.

Energy Wars and Social Change

LUTHER P. GERLACH

"You should talk to some of those Minnesota people protesting power lines on your way back to Minneapolis," the organizer in the Bismarck office of the United Plainsmen told me one day late in August 1974. He showed me a clipping from the *Fargo Forum* of that week and explained: "According to this article, people in Grant County in western Minnesota have formed a group they call 'No Power Lines' to fight construction of a high-voltage DC power line through their area from a thousand-megawatt plant two rural cooperative associations are building in Underwood—that's in central North Dakota." He pointed to his big map. "That's here where all the lignite is mined. Apparently the line will go to a station near Minneapolis where it will be converted to AC and be put into the grid."

The organizer and other participants in the United Plainsmen had already described how through this organization they and other groups of farmers, ranchers, and townsfolk in North Dakota were struggling to stop, or at least control, the construction and operation of such power plants, as well as the strip mining of the lignite used to fuel them. He explained that they worried that this development would hurt their land, interrupt underground flow of water, pollute their air, and bring in so many newcomers with different values and objectives that their traditional way of living would be upset. Earlier that week, officials in various energy-developing industries working in North Dakota had explained to me how the development of these fossil resources would help free the region from dollar-destroying dependence on Arab oil and bring in jobs to revitalize dying rural towns. They and government officials also explained that public participation in making decisions about the siting of energy facilities would protect the people and their local values.

I had come to North Dakota both to observe local conditions and to interview these farmers, ranchers, miners, energy developers and resisters, government officials, and technical experts who represented the conflicting positions on the development of energy resources in this area. Extrapolating from our model and from concepts of structure and function of social movements and their role in generating or resisting change

(Gerlach and Hine 1970, 1973), and from our studies of energy issues (Gerlach and Eide 1975; Gerlach 1976; Gerlach and Palmer 1978), I had identified the situation in Minnesota and North Dakota as a possibly productive case study. I expected that relations between North Dakotans and Minnesotans would be relatively representative of relations between energy have and have-not regions across America and around the world.

I believed that studying how people and groups in Minnesota and North Dakota would act and interact in respect to energy development would help me learn how evolving technologies of energy development would generate new systems of social-political integration, environmental adaptation, and cultural conceptualization.

Much of my earlier research and analysis had focused on the ways people mobilize into social movements. The process has several steps. Characteristically they (1) build an *organization* which pulls people into joint venture over an increasing area, while maintaining the flexibility, entrepreneurship, independence, and innovation characteristic of individualistic pursuit. They (2) develop and spread a motivating, integrating, and legitimating ideology that plays upon and generates discontent. Ideology helps mobilize people to counter-action by telling them they have the duty and the right to fight back and the power to win. Such mobilized groups (3) *recruit* new participants from as broad a base as possible. They (4) commit participants to work hard and effectively for the purposes of the movement and to persist in such involvement for months or even years. Finally, the groups develop (5) a sense of in-groupness or we-groupness among participants against all others. In this case study the outgroup is composed of the energy developers, who are increasingly perceived as a dangerous, unethical, immoral *opposition* whose activities can be attacked as illegitimate. These characteristics compose an interrelated and dynamic process. This process logically begins as people see some sort of threat or challenge. It is when people begin organizing in groups and spreading the word that they develop, learn, and communicate ideas about the threat or challenge and about ways to achieve their objectives. As people begin organizing and communicating, indicators of a rising social movement appear.

My colleagues and I have found the organization of movements to be strikingly different from the centralized, bureaucratic organization of established orders or conventional voluntary associations. We have also found it to be quite different from the model of a single charismatic leader (Moorehead 1960) commanding a mass of blindly following true believers (Hoffer 1965). In the movements I have studied, participants come together in many different groups or segments, and they generate many different leaders. The groups proliferate, sometimes dividing, sometimes recombining, bubbling up and dying away, fading in and out of view, leaders teaching and leading because they know how to listen and follow, usually careful to be no more than "first among equals." Groups and leaders vary in their styles, composition, tactics, specific goals, degree of militancy, and formality. Since the segments are so autonomous, any can survive the elimination or error of others.

Yet these various segments and leaders are not simply unconnected fragments which can be played against each other. While *segmented* and *polycentric,* they are also *integrated* in *networks.* I have found it convenient to use the acronym SPIN to summarize this. Interacting as equals rather than as links in a formal chain of command, participants and groups in such SPIN organization collaborate and exchange information in ways which build and maintain these networks. Networking is also facilitated as some people participate in more than one group, as some use or develop personal ties with participants in other groups, or as some leaders crisscross the network like traveling evangelists. These organizational characteristics enable the parts of the movement to come together to coordinate action and mass effort against a common opposition, yet at the same time to respond flexibly to their specific conditions, to innovate, and to survive the failure of some of the parts. Like a segmentary lineage system (Sahlins 1961), SPIN is admirably adapted to expand into and control new territories, but for SPIN the territories are as much cultural as spatial. Movements quickly challenge and often change established ideas.

Ideology is generated and used as the various segments of the movement are born and grow and conflict with the opposition. Ideology is a weapon employed by participants in the movement as they go out to witness to and recruit newcomers into their groups. It is around specific differences in ideology that groups may split or start anew. Yet there is a basic set of ideological premises that helps glue all the groups together. Ideological development then becomes an indicator of the genesis and evolution of movements.

By acting in movement groups and sharing and promoting movement ideology, participants face censure, ridicule, economic sanctions, and physical risk from established orders. Throughout the course of movement development there are various points at which one can ask if these control methods will succeed in suppressing individual participants and stop the movement altogether, or if instead they will provide sufficient risk to radicalize and commit participants to deeper belief and action without destroying them. In the United States established orders have been found to escalate counter-measures slowly enough so that they customarily increase rather than suppress commitment. We have been able to identify points in the development of a movement in which organization, recruitment, ideology, opposition, and commitment begin interacting so dynamically that anything the established order does will make the movement grow. For example, if the established order admits that it is wrong and gives in to the movement's demands, then the movement will grow and expand. If the established order says that the movement has gone far enough and applies force to control it, this will provide the risk necessary for the further commitment of the participants. If the force is strong enough to be effective it will seem excessive to the general public so that they will side with the movement as underdogs. If the established order does nothing, the movement will see this as weakness and also grow. It is predictable that established orders confronted by a SPIN organization will denigrate it as disorganized and chaotic and will show rising frustration in their inability to predict what it will do, to control it, or to negotiate with it. Just when an established order has identified some groups and leaders and found ways to work with these, new ones rise and move to the front, increasing demands and often stimulating the others to more militant action.

Our research has not been as successful in determining what brings about the decline and fall of a movement. One major study that attempts to do just this argues that it takes a counter-movement (Meisel 1966). In any event, movements do generate significant social change. Evidence has led my colleagues and me to argue that the change produced by social movements active in our society during the last decade has been adaptive (Gerlach and Hine 1973).

The model used in this work is one of structure, function, and process, rather than one of root cause. Like Wilson (1973) and as we have explained elsewhere (Gerlach and Hine 1970), we have found that the more conventional models are not useful (Wallace 1956; Hoffer 1965; Linton 1943). These models seek to attribute the genesis of movements to the push of presumed preconditions of social, psychological, or economic deprivation or disorganization. In our studies we have not been able to determine preconditions or combinations of preconditions and precipitators necessary or sufficient to cause a movement. We have, however, made some useful guesses about the conditions which will *facilitate* the rise and growth of movements. The facilitating conditions provide a kind of field or arena in which to look for the early indicators of movement organization and ideology. If we observe a SPIN-like organization and see ideas proliferating that upset the established order, if we observe the established order having trouble understanding this and trying to control it, and if we see evidence of risk and commitment among participants, we can identify this as an operating social movement which seems to generate the very conditons that help it grow. When the movement factors of SPIN organization, ideology, recruitment, commitment, and opposition emerge and begin to interact with established orders, then Maruyama's (1965) model of mutual causal deviation amplification applies: movement factors and facilitating conditions interact in positive feedback to make the movement continue to grow and to change established orders.

We developed our models and approach chiefly by studying the Charismatic Renewal and Black Power movements, which were in full swing when we began our research in the 1960s. We first used them to anticipate the rise of a new movement when, in 1967, we identified neoconservation as "participatory ecology" or the environmental movement.

When I evaluated areas of future conflict and change in 1973, I saw that the arena holding the most potential for facilitating the rise of a new movement was the arena of energy shortage and development. This was especially true because of the ways government and technocratic elites, inspired or changed by the environmental movement's ideas, would seek to manage energy development, energy resources, and public "choices." Trends indicated that Minnesota and other states poor in energy would come to rely increasingly on electricity and eventually on synthetic gas and fuel produced from lignite and coal mines and minemouth plants in the Northern Great Plains states of North Dakota, Montana, and Wyoming to be distributed over long transmission and pipe lines. This technological development, however, held great potential for social stress, for example in the clash of values between local independence and regional interdependence, need-for-growth and no-growth ideologies and between large scale technological solutions and "appropriate technology" ideals. That is why I had come to the lignite fields of North Dakota to begin looking at the problem.

Since the process of public hearing and site selection provided for in a new Minnesota state siting law seemed to require that alternative locations be considered and that people from very diverse social groups be urged to participate in the hearings, I predicted that even more people than usual would be stimulated to activity. People would be upset about the actual or threatened impact of the development and also about the technocratic, systemic process by which its impact was assessed, the alternatives considered, and sites chosen. It seemed highly probable that a no-win situation, a dilemma, would be created. At the time of my visit people resisting energy development in North Dakota seemed to have stabilized their organization, placing reliance on a paid organizer (the man with whom I had spoken in the Bismarck office of the United Plainsmen) who was to coordinate their efforts and deal with the established order. It did not seem, therefore, that their actions would develop into a social movement. What about Minnesota?

En route to Minneapolis from North Dakota, I sought out the No Power Lines (NPL) people. Jim Nelson, the reported spokesman, was not there. He had just left with his wife to visit North Dakota to establish contact with the United Plainsmen and any others fighting power plants and lines. Jim's mother and father were home, however, and I spoke with them. In calm and measured tones they explained that Jim had a master's degree in physics, had worked in the aerospace industry near Boston, and had recently returned to help his father farm the family's eight hundred acres. Then eagerly they laid out an array of clippings, articles, and documents about power lines, grid systems, and energy matters, and reports warning of possible health and safety hazards from high voltage transmission lines. They talked about the dangers of such a line, how it interferes with farming, with aerial spraying, with good living on the land they love. They explained how Jim apparently had caught the power company in an underhanded move designed to push through the line without going through the new hearing process. They sent me on to speak with others in NPL, neighbors who would probably see the line over or near their prime agricultural land if the "company" put it where it wanted to.

One of these early resisters was a farm wife who had a degree in social work. Another was an engineer who had left Grant County to be educated, serve in the military, and become an executive in the aerospace industry in California. He came back to buy land for a summer place near the three-generation family spread farmed by his brother. Another was a former deputy chief of the Minnesota Pollution Control Agency who also had decided to return to the country. Like the Nelsons, they laid out an ideology to motivate and legitimate further action and they made clear their hostility toward the builders of the line. For example, they referred to the builders as a power "company" rather than as a joint venture of rural electric cooperative associations (which calls itself the CU or Cooperative United project). The resisters implied that the cooperatives were just trying to make profits and grow big at the expense of farmers instead of helping meet their real energy needs.

Other studies had shown me how established orders characteristically explain movements in terms of the specific psychological or socioeconomic characteristics of presumed key leaders of groups which at any one time are giving them trouble. It did not surprise me that in this case cooperative executives, media reporters, and government officials, in their quest for explanations for the militant attack on what they considered to be a necessary and safe project, initially attributed the action of these people to their high level of education and their supposed utopian vision of return to a simpler life in the country.

Within a few months, however, other groups were springing up to fight the line in other counties likely to be affected by its presence. People of varied backgrounds were rising to lead and participate in such groups as Keep Towers Out, Save Our Countryside, Towers Out of Pope, and Preserve Grant and Traverse Counties.

Most of the resisters in all of the counties were long-established and relatively successful farmers. At first most were at least middle-aged but as militant action burgeoned, many more younger farmers entered the struggle. In some areas most resisters have been German Catholics, in other areas most have been Scandinavian Lutherans. Few are educated beyond college, but most have finished high school and some have gone on to college or have taken course work in technical or agricultural programs. Predictably, established orders responded to the attacks of these new groups by continuing to focus on presumed specific characteristics, but now the complaint was their low level of education, rural backwardness, German Catholic clannishness, or Scandinavian stubbornness.

The movement has kept alive, grown, declined and grown again through a series of successes and reverses. During the first four years of its life, its participants have continued to create new groups for new purposes: for instance, to incorporate new allies, to recruit more broadly, to deal with divisions over tactics and opinions, or to respond to new problems. In this and other ways this movement has shown an ability to adapt rapidly to changing conditions and needs and, above all, to the actions of established orders. In many ways it has forced CU and government to respond to its challenges.

CU originally planned, for example, to get their right of way for the line in traditional fashion, negotiating separately with local landowners and securing approval from local government without coming under the new state-level siting process. They began operations before the effective date of the new state law. They were therefore excluded from it by the "savings" or "grandfather" clause. Immediate resistance from NPL and other resister groups block them, however, by persuading local governments to take various actions, including a vote in one county to "zone out" the line. CU then decided that it would probably take less time and be more efficient if they obtained a route through the state process.

The 1973 law concerning the siting of transmission lines provided for a process of public hearings by the new Minnesota Environmental

Quality Council (EQC, since renamed Environmental Quality Board) to locate first a corridor and then a route for the line. Later legislation provided that in addition to this process, the new Minnesota Energy Agency must conduct hearings to determine if the line was needed to serve the public. CU felt sure that they would prove need and that the route granted would be close enough to the one they preferred.

As I anticipated, when people within this broad area of corridor and route study were urged to participate in the state process, increasing numbers came to ask questions, then to defend their interests, and then to resist the whole project. They joined existing resistance groups or formed their own, since it was apparent that if people did not organize they would lose to those who did. CU implied that people were creating selfish pressure groups simply to have the line moved onto the property of others. Resisters responded with organization and ideology, as we thought they would. They said that CU was trying to turn farmers against each other in order to "pick them off, one by one." They went out with renewed effort to urge people across west central Minnesota to organize locally to oppose the line. When CU asked where people expected to get the energy they needed if no one wanted the line, the resisters challenged need. This was done in spite of the fact that the food production practices many farmers have found necessary for growth, and thus economic survival, increasingly depend upon low cost electrical energy. It was logical for them to urge that CU stop being so rigid and instead seek other ways to transmit the energy, or use energy more efficiently. Pursuit of alternatives began with suggestions to put the line underground, along railroad and highway rights of way, or to put it through state parks or wildlife areas over environmental objections. Eventually some resisters collaborated with urban activists to experiment with ways to send electricity without wires or to build solar, wind, or methane systems.

Consistent with our predictions, the adversarial nature of the hearing process and the resisters' interaction with and perception of the CU lawyers and state officials combined to push the movement of resistance forward. As the resisters prepared for the hearings and then rehashed their experiences with their fellows, they helped interweave their groups into expanding networks, developing and communicating their ideology. Then, as they presented testimony and stood up to tough cross-examination by lawyers who seemed to want to discredit them, they advanced their commitment.

Even though the hearing process was solidifying the opposition, the authorities could not terminate or significantly alter it because this would create more resistance, open them to lawsuits, and legitimate the movement even more. This was an example of positive feedback—anything done to control the movement would actually help it grow.

In June 1976, the EQC voted to grant CU a permit for the construction of the line generally along or near their preferred route. As could be expected, the resisters were angrier than ever. They expected this verdict but could not accept it. They left the hearing at the state capitol with some of their leaders warning that there would be violence when CU tried to survey and build.

Resisters did act to chase away right-of-way agents seeking easements and to interfere with the work of surveyors seeking to lay out the path of the line. While some resisters had anticipated that actions of this sort would occur, these were at first unplanned and spontaneous. People watched the surveyors with mounting anger, and then in one place after another someone blocked their line of sight with farm equipment or protest signs, interfered with their communications by running chain saws, or stood in the way of equipment. Then quickly the resisters' communication network went into action: phones and CB radios hummed, and the people gathered. New groups and leaders quickly rose, with leadership vested in the one who first blocked the survey crew, the one who best interacted with the sheriff and deputies who came to prevent fighting, or the one who made the best case before the TV news cameras.

Soon the old groups which carried the fight through the hearing process returned to the fray and called others from their circle of kinfolk and friends to the cause. In these ways many different types of people throughout the affected counties came out to help, even if the final routing had put the line far away from them, or even if they had never been threatened by it.

The resisters said that they, not CU, were in the right. They declared eminent domain immoral and unjust, and said it was illegitimate to use deputy sheriffs to enforce the construction permit. It was their land and no one had the right to force them to accept surveyors or power lines on it. Local public opinion mounted on the side of the resisters. It is not surprising that the sheriffs were reluctant to use force on people whom they considered to be otherwise good and law-abiding. In addition, the protesters were neighbors who could vote them into or out of office. Similarly, one county attorney resigned rather than prosecute those who would be arrested for breaking this law. The state had created the problem, these local officials said, with its siting process. The state had negated actions by the counties to zone out or question the line, so the state ought to handle the problem of enforcement. The fragile system of what the Minnesota Department of Public Safety calls "voluntary compliance" was in jeopardy. As I had expected, the resisters found historical precedent and symbols for their actions. They likened their resistance to the struggle by North American colonists against the British and King George. In the many months to come they were to use again and again symbols of this struggle for independence. Jenks's farm, where they stood against surveyors in 1976 and early 1977, was called "Constitution Hill," and Lowry Town Hall, where they gathered in weekly or daily meetings in 1977 and 1978 to plan tactics and sally forth against surveyors and builders, was called "Bunker Hill." They carried the American flag proudly in their marches, demonstrations, and confrontations and waved it in front of surveyors' transits to block their line of sight. They also referred to the way Americans broke laws they considered unjust to fight for civil rights and later to fight against the war in Viet Nam, even though most admitted that in the sixties and early seventies they did not agree with such tactics.

As this conflict in the fields first developed through the summer and fall of 1976, it seemed only a matter of time before the state would consider calling out the National Guard or the state troopers. Many people worried about this. They certainly worried about the fact that conflict could lead to bloody encounters between guardsmen and farmers, and perhaps that any such conflict in an election year could jeopardize state and national political careers.

Probably for this reason each time mounting tension appeared to force a showdown that would mean calling out guards or troopers, ways were found to back away and let tempers cool. State government passed the problem back to the local level. For example, when one district judge ordered a county sheriff to hire enough deputies from around the state and region, the sheriff found good reasons why this hiring and subsequent training would take many months. While the court in one district found that construction should go on and resistance was illegal, a court in another district restrained construction while it considered a strong legal point brought before it by resisters.

It is difficult to summarize all of the ensuing events. It seems so complex in retrospect. Perhaps it should have seemed even more confusing as it developed, for certainly my notes show that things were happening in rapid succession, and often simultaneously. At the time we were able to anticipate most specific moves. I certainly had the feeling that this was all being played out as if it were a drama—a tragedy whose script was already written. Much of it would continue the next year, with a repetition of scenes and actors, but with new and more dramatic elements.

I had expected, for example, that attempts would be made by various parties to mediate this dispute. It seemed to be turning into the kind of classic standoff and threat to public order that characteristically brings forth attempts by third parties to seek settlement. I also recognized that neither side had the desire to compromise. CU did not really believe that it could ever lose because the law was officially on its side; it had the route, it could show that the line was needed, and it could expect that when the chips were down the government would back it up with sufficient legal force. The resisters were the underdogs, but they had come to believe that right was on their side and that ultimately the government would agree. In any event they had the commitment to fight against all odds.

It made sense that the church would seek to mediate. At the time I did not know enough about the religious structure of the area to anticipate that it would be the Roman Catholic bishop who would be the first to act. I learned after he sat down with resisters and CU officials to mediate the dispute that he was already a strong advocate of the rural life movement and the maintenance of the family farm. When he said that he felt the farmers had not been treated fairly and that energy development must not be at the expense of family farming, it was not surprising that CU felt he was biased. For this and other reasons the mediation effort failed. Mediation involving SPIN organization is always going to be difficult.

It can be predicted that negotiators, as well as the heads of any formal organization, will feel that the movement should delegate one or a small number of leaders to represent the movement and to be empowered to make and keep agreements. But we know that SPIN usually does not work this way, especially when the movement is growing and when groups are still forming or dividing. As the power line movement and its conflict with CU and then government and law enforcement continued, more attempts were made by churches, by the new governor, and then by other organizations to mediate the dispute. Throughout all of this, the organization and dynamics of SPIN kept frustrating the would-be negotiators.

In January, Rudy Perpich took over as governor of Minnesota when Wendell Anderson left this office to move into the senate position vacated as Walter Mondale shifted to vice-president. Perpich tried to resolve the conflict by going out to meet the farmers face to face. He had a reputation as a populist. This personal visitation made sense: he hoped that it would establish him as the man in charge, the man who knew what was going on first hand, not through a previous governor's appointees. His visit raised expectations on all sides. Judging from our observations of him among the resisters as well as on television and in press releases, he seemed to warm to the resisters. The farmers thought he could and would help them. What the farmers wanted was to stop the line. What the new governor wanted, apparently, was a compromise. At his urging, state legislators, well aware and afraid of the potential for conflict over construction of the line, held special hearings on the issue. They heard resisters as well as CU officials and farmers from other areas who felt they needed the electricity from the proposed line. Based on this and many other sessions in which resisters contributed, the legislature considered legislation to amend the 1973 siting law.

The governor, meanwhile, also sought to get the cooperatives and the resisters to negotiate some type of settlement. First he tried to do this himself; then he brought in a professional mediator from New York City recommended by the American Arbitration Association. Later he again tried personally to serve as the middle man. To facilitate such mediation, he also proposed that a science court be established to consider, and presumably to determine, whether the line would or would not impose a health hazard.

I was not surprised that these attempts failed. CU continued to believe that it was in the right, that the law was on its side, and that it was somehow a violation of principle to keep listening to the complaints of resisters. CU felt that resisters should abide by the legal decision and that negotiating with them was reinforcing their unfounded belief that they could stop the line and that it should be stopped. It seemed as if CU itself was crusading for a cause. On the other side, it seems that the resisters did interpret quest for negotiation as a sign that they were putting pressure on government and that the cooperatives might be defeated. Few of the resisters, if any, were willing to make, or admit that they would make, concessions.

The governor and the mediator were frustrated in their attempts to identify and work with a selected sample of resisters who could represent all of the others and make agreements other than agreements to stop or delay construction of the line. The governor was not the first person to feel that in negotiating with a SPIN organization, "just when we had agreements, the leadership changed." In movements of this type, leadership and membership are usually in flux yet also usually ready to unite to affirm root principles or to face common threat to survival.

Resisters had at this point come together again as members of named groups under larger umbrella organizations to present their case to the governor, and then the legislature, at mass meetings. They also put together small task forces to press home their arguments at the state capitol in numerous legislative committee sessions on power line siting. Similarly, they had organized in both formal and ad hoc groups to carry their fight through the courts where they were contesting actions of the developers and decisions of the state siting process and, eventually, defending themselves from the many law suits that emerged from their attempts to stop surveying and construction in the fields.

In the fall of 1977 the resisters' cause seemed absolutely lost on all legislative and legal fronts, as it had many times before. The previous spring the legislature had amended the siting law to answer many of the resisters' complaints that the law was not fair to farmers. It provided, for example, that wildlife management areas owned by the state could not be given preference over cropland in evaluating alternatives for routing lines, that landowners receive an annual share of the taxes the utilities would pay on the facilities, and that wherever possible, easements should follow section lines instead of crossing agricultural land diagonally. This new legislation, however, could not be applied retroactively, according to the state constitution.

When hearings were held during the fall on the rules for implementing this revised statute, resisters used them as a forum. They wanted to insure that the intent of the legislature regarding these matters be carried out in practice in the future and to point out that it was unjust that the revisions did not apply to their case. Meanwhile, on all levels the courts upheld the construction permit and found against all suits by resisters to stop, slow, or reroute construction. The state supreme court did, however, urge higher easement payments. Would the resisters now give in and accept the inevitable, secure at least in the belief that they had been heard and that they had had an impact on decisions about these issues in the future? Would they agree with the governor that he and the legislature and everyone else had, as he said in his 1977 state address, "gone the extra mile" to treat the protesters fairly? Would they say that the higher easements CU now seemed to be offering would be acceptable? I didn't think they would. I predicted that these actions and setbacks would reinforce their sense that they were right and that they must keep fighting (Gerlach 1978).

Resistance did continue. Resisters reechoed that it was a principle for which they were fighting, not simply higher easement payments. They felt that no one had yet proven to them that the line was safe. They were not appeased by CU's finding university specialists to monitor the line for ozone emissions. Many asked why they should be guinea pigs to see if a DC line of this size was safe. They continued to feel it was an injustice to be forced to accept the line. They declared that the legislature must make more fundamental change, like taking back the right of the utilities to use eminent domain.

Once again, when the resisters rallied in the fall of 1977, they came together in new groups, rooted in the old ones but extended to include many new supporters. By this time their antiline networks were overlapping with networks of people and groups organized to resist proposed construction of atomic and coal-fired power plants elsewhere in the state and across the border in Wisconsin. Further, their antiline networks were linking with networks of people and groups based in the Twin Cities and in various colleges in the area. These groups were advocates of alternative energy and alternative lifestyles, cooperating in distributing natural foods, and fighting for local control against a centralized urban renewal project. I anticipated such overlapping of interests and activities in spring 1977, as farmers collaborated with some of the people from the urban food cooperative in building a system to transmit and receive electricity without wires, using principles proposed in 1908 by Nicola Tesla. As I also had anticipated, in the winter of 1977–78, the resisters established links with Minnesota segments of the American Agricultural Movement. I expected this link to be stronger than proved to be the case.

In January 1978, when the power line resisters and their allies were again able to defy the local sheriffs and stop construction work, the governor of Minnesota dispatched over 150 state highway troopers to enforce the construction permit and protect the construction workers and surveyors. From January to late February, the resisters gathered for large rallies (which resembled the revival meetings we observed during our study of the Charismatic movement) and then marched out to confront surveyors and construction workers. Mostly they protested with symbolic display, proclaiming their right to demonstrate in spite of court orders they considered illegitimate. Time and again some stepped forward to cross the line set up by the troopers and thus to offer themselves for arrest. Almost always there was the threat of serious violence and bloodshed, and on several occasions people on both sides were hurt.

This mounting threat of violence and a massive gathering of thousands of resisters and supporters in the capitol again forced the legislature to ask what it could do and to consider declaring a moratorium until it could be demonstrated that the line was not a threat to the farmers' health and safety. It decided it could do nothing. Its hands were tied as much by previous decisions as by the lack of evidence that there were known significant health hazards. In short, the legislature was also constrained to follow the decision of the siting process, validated time and again by the courts. Some of the legislators asked the resisters to accept this, finally, and to work with government to promote energy conservation, alternative energy programs, and reforms in the siting and eminent domain laws so that a crisis like this could be avoided in the future.

The resisters expected a rebuff, but it still hurt them. It was one of their many disappointments. Once again they took to the fields, demonstrated, and broke trooper lines, and some were arrested. Commitment rose as risks rose. But the degree of violence and counter-violence also rose—and frightened many resisters. Were they creating something they could not control? Were they becoming as bad as the evil they were fighting? If the troopers sprayed a chemical deterrent, ostensibly to protect themselves, was it right that a few resisters rolled out in tractors to spray anhydrous ammonia?

How did the resisters and troopers themselves interpret and respond to this? When we went to the power line construction area the following week, we saw that though the resisters continue to go out to demonstrate before surveyors, they did not continue to cross trooper lines. They came close but at the last moment backed away. Their anger was as great as ever, but they were forming a consensus to deescalate. They led and the troopers responded, often seeming to misunderstand. Two troopers explained to me, for example, that the resisters went too far when they sprayed the ammonia but later commented that they were not making much of a point when they simply came out to look on while the surveyors worked. I guessed that the resisters had taken the initiative to back away from disaster, but I also guessed that the established order was not going to understand what it meant or what had happened.

The resisters decided to hold a great gathering of those who were fighting the line and those who were supporting or would support them. They called it a March for Justice, referring to their premise that their rights to their land and to free assembly to protest injustice had been abrogated. Many contributed to the development of this event, but key ideas sparking it were set forth by a person who was a leader of resistance efforts in some of the 1975 and 1976 state hearings. He had pulled back from the conflicts which followed the granting of the construction permit. The line never came close to his place, but he emerged again as a leader in this and following key events. Various groups got to work. New groups of supporters from local towns as well as other groups of urban supporters, a spokesman for Eastern coal mine strikers, American Agriculture Movement allies, and many others became involved. Network after network was mobilized. On 5 March 1978, at least seven thousand people participated in the giant March for Justice. It was held on a farmer's field across the county road from the field in which the construction company working for CU was putting together the girders of the steel towers which were to carry the transmission line.

Five days later, Friday, 10 March, about two hundred resisters met in Lowry, Minnesota, to discuss the future of their movement and to determine how they should now act. It seemed that most wanted new tactics to adapt to changing conditions. A small majority voted to change from tactics which deliberately courted arrest because those tactics cost too much and did not win enough support. Some argued it was better to find ways to defeat the line through more legal action by finding flaws in the regulations and their implementation.

The press, hurrying to get in a story, and later the governor, interpreted this to mean that the resisters were not going to protest construction except within the political system. The governor announced that he was recalling the troopers.

By Sunday, 12 March, some of the resisters were declaring that the reporters and others had misinterpreted their decision. They were marching on the capitol in another demonstration on Wednesday and would not rule out future civil disobedience in the fields.

Will the struggle continue? Probably. The established order still does not know how to cope with the movement, especially its SPIN organization. It continues to be thwarted by the movement's ability to turn setbacks and what otherwise would be effective control into the risk and experience that commit people to the cause of resistance and change.

People involved in or affected by these movements have generally agreed that the models used here give them understanding of how movements work and how established orders respond to them. Most have learned that my co-workers and I have been able to anticipate steps in the unfolding of these movements. Both movements and established orders have their own interpretations of what is happening, what it means, why it has begun, and why it persists. Various theories of conspiracy and intimation of hidden purpose are common to both sides. Either is likely to suggest that somewhere at the root of the other's actions is some sort of master plan or conspiracy, or some secret purpose. It is as if each feels that somebody must be in control, somewhere, somehow. They search for solutions, and they imply that if I through my research project know enough to explain, predict, and lay out the dilemmas so clearly, I should be able to offer a solution. Established orders find little comfort in my description of the movements affecting them as a recurrent phenomenon proceeding in an understandable or predictable pattern. All they have for the moment is someone before them who can face their wrath or anguish as a kind of surrogate for the movement. They ask, "What good is an explanation or a prediction which implies that events will unfold no matter what anyone tries to do?"

Participants in movements have usually been willing to accept my analysis and communication of findings to the general public. They also accept the role of the press in getting their story out but often worry that it does not do a thorough job.

Energy developers and, frequently, government officials often say that movements such as the anti–power line movement are an irrational, unique intrusion into the procedures through which they could otherwise logically proceed step by step to produce and transmit energy to meet the needs they forecast or to manage the environmental tradeoffs and legitimate social concerns. While they would agree that protest is generally good in a free society, they seem to suggest for the case in question that it has gone too far. Energy developers accept problems like rising interest rates and fuel shortage as real, to be dealt with by normal financial or engineering operations. They accept the fact that Minnesota has no coal, oil, or natural gas of its own as geological reality. Although developers will complain about government red tape, they have come to accept dealing with regulatory bureaucracy as a regular and essentially controllable part of their operations. Their best hope, however, is to learn how to cope with, if not control, movements that resist their projects, challenge their forecasts, protest their rates, or protest shortages or inequities in the distribution of their products. My analysis suggests more movements which have opposite goals. In responding to one, established orders create the problems which then provoke another. The American Agriculture Movement, for example, is gaining strength in its demand for a fairer slice of the economic pie, while other groups seek to protect the slice they now have by fighting higher food costs and inflation generally. When gains from past movements are threatened, we may see a remobilization of these movements. The American system has characteristically resolved these conflicts with growth and expansion, but such growth and expansion has meant plentiful energy, a willingness to exploit our environment, and unspoiled space available for escape.

Can we then solve problems only by creating new ones? Is there no way to control this disturbing process and bring things back to normal? It is not surprising that when I present talks or programs on this subject with this kind of evidence and theory, people say that I am pessimistic, another one of those prophets of doomsday who feel we should just sit back and let ourselves be destroyed. I always respond by saying that I am optimistic. My reason, I tell the audience, is that I see all of this action and dilemma as the way Americans are evolving to a new level or form of society and culture. The new one won't necessarily be better than the old, but it will be different and, I presume, more adaptive. Movements, I then argue, function to innovate and inject new ideas into the system, to release people from the traps of conventional wisdom, and to create selective pressures that will generate new organization and culture. If I am given time I suggest, for example, that the dominant social organization of the future will be the very segmentary, polycentric, and networked system characteristic of social movements. I show that this SPIN organization is replacing centralized bureaucracies as people and institutions of all types adapt to new conditions, not the least of which is challenge by other social movements.

Together with colleagues (Hine 1977; Gerlach and Palmer 1978), I have described the shape of this process and how it works. SPIN, we say, is becoming the organization of joint ventures in resource development, of government and planning regulators, of technological elites, and of mediators, as well as of movements. It is the organization of the interaction of these networks. Central organization is dead or dying in its ability to control these interactions and processes. Where is the controlling center in settling the coal miners' strike, in establishing peace in the Middle East, in resolving the power line dispute, in achieving "detente" between energy developers and resisters, in establishing and enforcing a new energy policy? Indeed, where is the center of our cities, or are they not also segmentary, polycentric, and networked? Can it not be predicted that this will increase without our being able to gain the insights to control it? What would be the risks to our freedom and ability to explore new means of adapting if central bureaucracies really could predict and control us? It is, of course, possible that the real controls will be exerted by technocratic elites organized translocally and globally in SPIN. But that is another story.

NOTE

Research reported in this paper was funded by Northwest Area Foundation, St. Paul, Minnesota, and by the Office of Water Resources Research.

REFERENCES

Gerlach, Luther P., 1976. Developer, Register, Mediator and Manager Network in Conflict over Energy Development: Disintegration or a New Kind of Integration? Paper delivered at Annual Meeting of the American Political Science Association, Chicago, September 2–5. Proceedings on microfilm.

———, 1978. The Great Energy Standoff. *Natural History Magazine* 87: 22–32.

Gerlach, Luther P., and Paul Eide, 1975. Truckers' Shutdown: Social Response to Resource Shortage. 16mm sound/color film. Media Resources Department, University of Minnesota.

Gerlach, Luther P., and Virginia H. Hine, 1970. *People, Power, Change: Movements of Social Transformation* (Indianapolis: Bobbs-Merrill).

————, 1973. *Lifeway Leap: The Dynamics of Change in America* (Minneapolis: University of Minnesota Press).

Gerlach, Luther P., and Gary Palmer, 1978. Global Adaptation through Evolving Interdependence. In *Handbook of Organizational Design,* Paul C. Nystrom and William H. Starbuck, eds. (Amsterdam: Elsevier Scientific Publishing). In press.

Hine, Virginia H., 1977. The Basic Paradigm of a Future Socio-Cultural System. *World Issues* April–May: 19–22.

Hoffer, Eric, 1965. *The True Believer* (New York: Harper and Row).

Linton, Ralph, 1943. Nativistic Movements. *American Anthropologist* 45: 230–40.

Maruyama, Margorah, 1965. The Second Cybernetics: Deviation Amplifying Mutual Causal Processes. *American Scientist* 51: 164–79.

Meisel, James H., 1966. *Counter-Revolution: How Revolutions Die* (New York: Atherton Press).

Moorehead, Alan, 1960. The Moslem Revolt. In *The White Nile* (New York: Dell Books), pp. 222–25.

Sahlins, Marshall D., 1961. The Segmentary Lineage: An Organization of Predatory Expansion. *American Anthropologist* 63: 322–45.

Wallace, Anthony F. C., 1956. Revitalization Movements. *American Anthropologist* 56: 264–81.

Wilson, John, 1973. *Introduction to Social Movements* (New York: Basic Books).

Revolution, Salvation, Extermination: The Future of Millenarianism in Brazil

PATRICIA R. PESSAR

This chapter differs from many in the collection.[1] The difference results from the difficulties inherent in making use of the theory and methodology available to the symbolic anthropologist interested in the task of prediction. There are essentially two major problems. The first is the problem of assigning causality. In the famous case of the relation between the Protestant ethic and the rise of capitalism, for example, Weber saw the symbol system as the independent variable, while for others it was the product of already emergent industrial technology and new social relations.[2] As a symbolic anthropologist, I find myself in a quandary when faced with the task of prediction. Following in the tradition of Geertz and Turner, I find it best to posit a dialectical relationship between symbol system and social system rather than to assign to one a causal function. While this dialectical approach to change proves helpful in interpreting, ex post facto, how changes in one system may have effected transformations in the other, it creates difficulties in predicting whether and how a modification in one system will affect the other.[3]

Another problem facing the symbolic anthropologist interested in predicting change is the absence of methodologies suited to the task. This lack may be traced both to the theoretical problem of determining independent and dependent variables and to the position of antipositivism assumed by many symbolists (Firth 1973). Some of the finest work performed by symbolists, in my opinion, has been to interpret symbolic forms in their own right, in terms of their own internal logic. A byproduct of this work has been the construction of sophisticated methodologies for the synchronic study of symbol systems. Far too little energy has been spent in creating methodologies to explain and to predict transformations in symbol systems.

The contributors to this collection were requested to present material suggesting the strengths and weaknesses of their chosen analytic approaches to the goal of prediction. I will be analyzing Brazilian millenarianism[4] from three perspectives available to the symbolic anthropologist. I will first employ a structural approach, follow it with a cultural analysis in which domains of meaning are described and inter-related, and conclude with what might be called an instrumental approach. Here the relationship between symbols and power will be probed.

I was guided into the realm of prediction by a statement by the philosopher of science, H. R. Harré. He advised, "Take care of the explanations and predictions will look after themselves" (Harré 1971: 581). This optimistic counsel implies that explanation will necessitate the formulation of a more adequate theory and lead to subsequent predictions to test the viability of the theory. The history of millenarian analysis has followed in opposite fashion. Explanations have grown out of, and have reinforced, existing theories, which have unfortunately tended to be functionalist ones. Millenarianism and other aspects of society have been explained by their functions, that is by their effects. Analysts have arrived at teleological explanations grounded in an organic theory of society, but an underlying causal mechanism, equivalent to that of natural selection in the theory of evolution, has never been formulated. As for prediction, functionalist explanations of millenarianism do not account for why millenarianism occurs in one social group suffering from relative deprivation (Aberle 1962) or mazeway disorientation (Wallace 1961) and not among other populations experiencing similar hardships.

I believe an adequate explanation of any social phenomenon must include a consideration of man as a self-reflexive being. If this charge is taken seriously, it means that prediction becomes more difficult as we disavow overly simple, positivist explanations of social action and replace them with theories and explanations that allow for both regularity and indeterminacy. I leave to the future the task of constructing a theory that incorporates the individual, culture, and society and will allow the prediction of the outcome of complex sociocultural relationships like that between millenarian beliefs and actions and politics in Brazil. Because of the lack of such a theory, the explanation formulated in this paper will allow only an approximation of the goal of prediction. In broadly conceiving of the relationship between millenarianism and certain features of the Northeast Brazilian cultural system and the Brazilian political economy, I have been able to isolate the potentials for the limitations on the contribution of millenarian beliefs and actions to future rebellion or revolution. This has allowed me to speculate on the alternatives for action afforded by millenarianism should specific changes occur in either the cultural or politico-economic systems, or both. These alternatives range from accommodation to revolution.

THE MILLENARIAN PARADIGM:
A STRUCTURAL ANALYSIS

Millenarianism has been described as an ideology of the oppressed by social scientists who have come to view millenarianism as one of the few political options available to those groups that are formally excluded from political decision making and resource distribution (Lanternari 1963; Hobsbawm 1959; Worsley 1957). Millenarianism is viewed by the analysts as a vehicle for organizing and mobilizing individuals to demand a more equitable distribution of resources, or as a vehicle for reconstituting internal and external political relationships, or both. While this approach has proved illuminating, its proponents have failed to analyze how millenarian beliefs may contribute to these political outcomes.

Repeatedly in the studies of millenarianism, the symbolic content and structure of these beliefs and symbols have been left unconsidered. The millenarian symbols are thus quite mechanistically "explained" by nonsymbolic contexts of experience. They are viewed as masking the true economic, political, and social issues—millenarianism being the only symbolic idiom available to an unsophisticated group. Unfortunately, by approaching millenarianism as an epiphenomenon, analysts have failed to investigate the elements and principles that render millenarian beliefs effective in motivating political action. Having isolated and analyzed the conceptual units and structural properties which characterize millenarian ideologies, I am inclined to view millenarianism as an agent rather than a mere reflector of change. Briefly I will trace the steps of my analysis, upon which this claim is based.

One of the most striking and least analyzed features of millenarian ideologies is their highly dramatic structure.[5] The dramatic content and structure contributes to the seductiveness of millenarianism as a vehicle about which people may identify and engage in creativity. Applying Burke's model for dramatic analysis of action to millenarian ideologies, the following pentad results:

Scene: Society, Heaven, and Hell[6]
Act: Salvation
Actors: The Supernatural, the Messiah, the Antichrist and his followers, the Chosen
Agency: Separation, Inversion, Obedience to the leader and his ideology, the Apocalypse
Purpose: The Millennium, Negation of process and structure, Salvation

The dramatic, dialectic structure from dominant order (thesis) through separation and liminality (antitheses) to the climax—eternal *communitas* (synthesis)—certainly would appear to be capable of seducing marginal individuals to identify with and act with reference to this drama. So too, the millennial symbols have the capacity to excite people to become committed—both on the conscious and unconscious levels—to the leader and his ideology. The symbols are psychologically rich in expectations for expiation, purification, liberation, and perfection. During the liminal phase one is freed from old structures and from the evil, repressive authority, which symbolizes and creates this structure. The climax is the millennium—a symbolic return to a state of innocence and eternal well-being.

Almost all millenarian ideologies categorize cultural and social life into binary opposites. Beliefs and institutions are commonly conceptualized as either good or evil. For example, a pamphlet distributed in 1534 by the Anabaptists reads:

> Amongst us God—to whom be eternal praise and thanks—has
> restored community, as it was in the beginning and as befits the Saints
> of God. . . . Accordingly, everything which has served the purposes of
> selfseeking and private property, such as buying and selling, working for
> money, taking interest and practising usury—even at the expense of
> unbelievers—or eating and drinking the sweat of the poor (that is, making
> one's own people and fellow-creatures work so that one can grow fat)
> and indeed everything which offends against love—all such things are
> abolished amongst us by the power of love and community. And knowing
> that God now desires to abolish such abominations, we would die rather
> than turn to them. (Cohn 1961: 266)

Wallace (1961) has argued that revitalization movements arise during periods of "uncoordinated cultural change." Prior to joining the movement, followers are said to view the world as unpredictable and without meaning. Wallace concludes that these times demand the "formulation of a code" to order these changes, render them meaningful, and to direct ameliorative actions. It is my contention that one of the properties of millenarian ideologies—the division of reality into binary opposites—reveals that a chaotic reality can be symbolically categorized and comprehended. In addition, it would appear from accounts of millenarian movements that this ordering may promote psychological, social, and cultural integration.

Nonetheless, it is easy to envision that the adoption and elaboration of a dualistic reality, based paradigmatically upon good and evil, might prove static and contribute to increased passivity. Following Turner's (1967, 1974) and Douglas's (1966) ideas about the property of liminality creating excitement, reflection, and the potential for innovative thought and action, I would suggest that resignation does not ensue.

While reality is dichotomized into binary oppositions, it is commonly an *inversion* of the order created and protected by the dominant class or the conquerors. For example, one Melanesian prophet predicted that "Papuans would become Whites, and the present Whites would have to clear the gardens while their former subjects ate rice" (Worsley 1957: 135). In Brazilian millenarian movements one similarly finds predictions of a time of the inversion of the present order. So the prophet of Canudos, Antonio Conselheiro, predicted:

> In 1896 a thousand flocks shall run from the seacoast to the back-lands; and then backlands will turn into a seacoast and seacoast into backlands.
> In 1897 there will be much pasturage and few trails, and one shepherd and one flock only.
> In 1898 there will be many hats and few heads.
> In 1899 the waters shall turn to blood, and the planet shall appear in the east with sun's ray, the bough shall find itself on the earth, and the earth shall find itself in heaven. (Da Cunha 1944: 135)

Millennial ideologies and social organizations may be likened to initiation rites. Turner relates:

> During the liminal period, neophytes are alternately forced and encouraged to think about their society, their cosmos, and the powers that generate and sustain them. Liminality may be partly described as a stage of reflection. In it those ideas, sentiments, and facts that had been hitherto for the neophytes bound up in configurations and accepted unthinkingly are, as it were, resolved into their constituents. These constituents are isolated and made into objects of reflection for the neophytes by such processes as componential exaggeration and dissociation by varying concomitants. The communication of *sacra* and other forms of esoteric instruction really involves three processes, though these should not be regarded as in series but as in parallel. The first is the reduction of culture into recognized components of factors; the second is their recombination in fantastic or monstrous patterns and shapes; and the third is their recombination in ways that make sense with regard to the new state and status that the neophyte will enter. (Turner 1967: 105–6)

In millenarianism we find an analogous three-part process. First there is a division of present experience into matched and opposing units of meaning. For example, see the discussion below of the thesis-antithesis in Brazilian society in the late 1800s and early 1900s. This division of reality is then inverted. That which is valued by those in power is rejected or reviled, and those meanings, values, and institutions which are denigrated by the powerful are prized and elaborated. An important outcome of this is the graphic demonstration of the mutability of existing social order. This realization, which is facilitated through the medium of symbols, may in certain contexts actively encourage individuals to oppose the upholders of society.[7] Most ideologies include a third stage, the "synthesis." Followers' enthusiasm not only results from the emotional liberation and excitement associated with symbolic inversion but is further stimulated by the belief that their actions will result in a spectacular climax. As described in millenarian ideologies, the millennium is envisioned as the final negation of all cultural and natural antagonisms, boundaries, and processes. This represents a great promise to those who suffer from being assigned to inferior categories. They are victims of racism, poverty, marginality, sickness, and early death.

In summary, millenarian ideologies have been commonly overlooked or dismissed as false consciousness by those most interested in the relationship between millenarianism and political action. In analyzing the structure of millenarian ideologies, one finds that their properties of binary opposition and inversion may contribute to political consciousness. In categorizing reality paradigmatically into good and evil, the immoral nature of the society created by the ruling group is starkly revealed. Further, under unstable or highly exploitative conditions, the structural properties and symbols of millenarian ideologies may contribute to the rebellious atmosphere by encouraging and orienting the dissatisfaction and despair of the populace. In situations where, for social structural or cultural reasons, people with a millenarian tradition have not produced social movements oriented toward rebellion or revolution, I would insist that the potential remains. Let us turn to the case of a society whose millenarian followers have never employed this antistructural potential.

MILLENARIANISM: A CULTURAL APPROACH

Brazil has been the site of recurrent millenarian movements. An incompletely explored aspect of these movements is their lack of significant political impact. A symbolic analysis of the Northeast Brazilian peasants' worldview and an investigation of the cultural domains of religion and politics contribute to an understanding of why millenarianism has assumed an accommodational rather than rebellious orientation.

For many analysts (Dela Cava 1968; Faco 1972) and for the Brazilian ruling class, millenarian movements are conceived to be political, but this is not the perception of the peasant followers. For the latter, millenarian activities are first and foremost concerned with salvation. This is a fact disregarded by most analysts, perhaps because it is for them part of the definition of millenarianism and thus not a topic for further explanation. The importance of salvation is also ignored as analysts search for causation or function at a systemic level of abstraction. They thus dismiss the statements informants make about their beliefs and behaviors. Such statements are often viewed as false consciousness or are considered to represent the obvious. Because of this dismissal of people's beliefs, millenarianism is often reduced to an epiphenomenon of the political and economic systems.

First I will place salvation in general, and millenarianism in particular, within the context of the Brazilian cultural system. The tremendous emphasis placed upon salvation can be traced to the period of conquest. The soldier conquerors came to Brazil with the ideological mission of creating a heaven on earth in the name of the "divine" Portuguese regent.[8] The missionaries carried a different mission for the Indians and African slaves. The message was heavily influenced by Jansenist theology and was well suited to a period of conquest and exploitation. The world and the flesh were evil. They were to be endured, not celebrated. The poor and oppressed were to glory in the similarity between their lives and the life of Christ. The fact that oriented their lives completely was the hope of salvation upon death. Resignation to one's condition and penitence for one's sins were understood by the poor to be the best agents for attaining salvation.[9] Should the devout Christian be deceived into thinking that salvation was probable, the fire and brimstone message of the popular *Missão Abreviada* warned that salvation was a gift that few would attain: "It is sure that only a few will be saved. . . . Sinner, turn from your deceptions; the assistances God will extend are numbered. . . . Extending beyond this number, you will not reach salvation, although you desire it; for in punishment for your obstinate nature, God must refuse you" (Goncalves Couto 1873: 399). Finally, apocalyptic beliefs were added to this world view of suffering and salvation. As many priests, prophets, and wandering troubadors warned, the time allotted to secure salvation was indeed short.

In such a cultural setting, it is understandable that individuals would seek those who would counsel them on the ways to attain salvation. Priests and friars might provide this service. Distance and demography, however, conspired against the Northeasterners. The average parish was 600 square miles and the average number of inhabitants per priest was over 16,600. Penitents who traveled the countryside also served as religious counselors. It was among this latter group that prophets and messiahs recurrently arose.

The lack of millenarian movements in many Spanish American societies with strong salvationist traditions indicates that there is not a one-to-one correspondence between a salvationist tradition and the development of millenarianism. Millenarianism may be viewed as one logical outcome of such a set of meanings and beliefs. Once millenarianism was established in Brazil, the concepts of the Antichrist and the Chosen became institutionalized in written and oral literature, and statuses, prophet and false prophet for instance, were assigned to individuals. Millenarianism then fed back into the belief system by further involving people in the preoccupation with and pursuit of salvation. Thus the many millenarianists I interviewed insisted that their involvement in these movements was motivated first and foremost by the goal of salvation.

While preoccupation with salvation and the hope of the imminent arrival of the millennium were always present, religious movements guided by these concerns were not. It would appear that the most favorable moments for the creation of such movements were periods of extreme social change. The years between 1875 and 1925 marked such a phase. These were years characterized by devastating drought, mass migration and dislocation, a decline of the traditional estate system, and a crisis of authority.

I neither view the millenarian movements that evolved during these and later years as representing Northeast society's correction of itself (Pereira de Queiroz 1965), nor do I interpret them as evolving out of a leader's recognition and correction of the psychic imbalance of his followers (Wallace 1961). Rather, I approach these movements from the perspective of very sane believers whose cultural system provides meanings and explanations for such disorder.

Northeasterners were beset by periods of extreme turmoil and suffering. Religion was the system of meaning available to the peasantry with which they could comprehend the causes and ramifications of this suffering. Why did so many turn to millenarianism? My answer is an inferential one. It is based upon the content of millennial tracts, interviews with millenarianists, and upon the interpretations I have heard expressed about the meaning of technological and social changes in contemporary Brazil. I would surmise that the massive, disorienting changes were interpreted as signs of the impending apocalypse. Millenarianism not only provided an excellent framework within which these changes could be ordered, but it was recognized as a vehicle for transforming the profound suffering into its opposite forever. People would accordingly have anticipated the arrival of the messiah and would have been inclined to attribute this status to individuals who demonstrated extraordinary qualities.

How then did millenarian ideologies provide meaning and orientation for many Northeast peasants? The symbolism and dialectical structure of the millenarian ideologies are well adapted to this task. Through ideological formulation, leaders and followers began the first step (the thesis) of ordering experience. The following tract from the Contestado movement is illustrative:

Dom Pedro the Second set forth
　　For Lisbon he was bound
And so the monarchy came to an end
　　And Brazil was left aground!

Backed up by the law
　　Those evil ones abound,
We keep the law of God,
　　They keep the law of the hound! [Satan]

Oh, wretched ones are they
　　When election comes around,
It's down with the law of God
　　And up with the law of the hound!

A mockery they make of marriage,
　　They'd have all true marriages cease
And have us all get married
　　By a justice of the peace!

The Anti-Christ was born
　　That he might govern Brazil,
But here is our Counselor [*Conselheiro*]
　　To save us from this ill!

Dom Sebastian our King
　　His visit we're awaitin'
And woe to that poor sinner then
　　Who is under the law of Satan! (Da Cunha, 1944: 163–64)

In dichotomizing society into good and evil, it must have become obvious to the millenarianists that divisions were being drawn, and evaluations being made, where they had hardly existed or had earlier been conceived of in opposite fashion. To many marginalized peasants, the sociocultural system of the late 1800s and early 1900s must have appeared something like this:

THESIS

"Good"	*"Evil"*
Dominant Class	Subordinate Class
Politics	Religion
City	Interior
Modernity	Tradition
Individualism	Community
Accumulation of Wealth	Charity
Honor	Suffering
Violence	Passivity
Antichrist	Christ

Following the dialectic logic of millenarian ideologies, the messiah taught that the hope for divine beneficence and the millennium existed only through the inversion of the presently evil and distorted way of life. What followed was ideological elaboration and the creation of sacred cities.

ANTITHESIS

"Good"	*"Evil"*
Subordinate Class	Dominant Class
Religion	Politics
Interior	City
Tradition	Modernity
Community	Individualism
Charity	Accumulation of Wealth
Suffering	Honor
Passivity	Violence
Christ	Antichrist

It is interesting that an occasional and, I would add, unintentioned outgrowth of this symbolic manipulation was the creation of stable, traditional communities like Santa Brigida in Bahia State. In millenarian communities organized around these principles of antithesis, the trends of social disaggregation, individuation, capital accumulation, and impersonal, rational authority were temporarily reversed. By turning to religion, and more particularly to millenarianism, some peasants were temporarily able to find refuge from the disturbing consequences of massive social change.

It may be asked whether this symbolic manipulation and creation of ideologies and communities represented political protest. An analyst may glean from the tracts of the Canudos movement and from critical comments about merchants and politicians attributed to the messianic figures Padre Cicero and Pedro Batista that these movements were reactionary. Their ideologies contained criticisms of the political and economic transitions toward bureaucratic, bourgeois society. Pedro Batista, for example, denounced the merchants who prospered at the expense of the poor. He advised, "The only type of negotiations that is justified is that between men and God." Both in belief and in deed, the millenarianists favored a return to the corporate peasant community overseen by one benevolent patron. While these movements were ideologically reactionary, the followers did not view their role as actively restructuring all of Brazilian society in this image. Their sacred communities were models of what might be divinely extended to all of Brazil, with the final synthesis of millenarian belief and action.

MILLENARIANISM AND THE CULTURE OF POLITICS

Many messiahs were proclaimed, and their religious ideology provided explanations for the disorder and discontent. Unlike messianic figures in other societies, their message did not inspire the poor to pursue political reorganization.

The speculation that cultural meanings held by Northeasterners might hamper the political potential of millenarian movements first arose when I spoke to the current leader of the Pedro Batista movement. She explained:

> I was with my Padrinho Pedor Batista in 1940 when we met a very extraordinary man. This was the only person I've ever seen my Padrinho take a blessing from! This man, who was filled with *misterio,* advised my Padrinho that his mission was not to enter into the world of men. His mission was another. This man said many would try to murder my Padrinho, but none could succeed. He warned that my Padrinho could only be undone if he entered into politics. . . . So when my Padrinho entered more and more into politics, I reminded him of the sacred man's message. But it was too late. He had entered into the world of men and had sacrificed his mission.

I was at first baffled by such criticism of Pedro Batista. It was, after all, by dint of political maneuvering with a political chief that Pedro Batista was able to settle his followers in 1945 and provide them with sufficient political security to pursue lives of penitence. Once safely settled, they benefited from his spiritual and material assistance. With the status of municipality secured by Pedro Batista in 1964, increased government funding and social services followed. I was later to conclude that much of the followers' discontent with the messianic leader could be traced to their beliefs about charisma *(misterio),* religion, and politics.

In my discussions with Northeasterners about the meanings associated with *misterio,* these features were stressed. *Misterio* belongs to the cultural domain of *religião* (religion). It is a god-given power to influence people and events positively. This power may be present from birth or may be acquired after a long period of suffering. *Misterio* is a power possessed in varying strengths by curers, penitents, prophets, and messianic leaders. It may or may not inhere in a priest. It is extremely rare for a politician to have *misterio.* In fact, the only politician consistently cited as having this power was a Brazilian president. Gertulio Vargas was said to be "a man of God whom politics and politicians destroyed." In pursuing this line of questioning, I found that politics was considered antithetical to *misterio.* Politics seemed to pollute, diminish, and possibly subvert this god-given power. The meanings held by the Northeasterners with whom I spoke pointed to a very different cultural conception of charisma from that formulated by Weber (1947) and Worsley (1957). *Misterio* was not conceived as a conduit between religion and politics. It pertained only to religion, and for my informants religion and politics were ideally two very discrete domains.

Religion is conceived as an arena for formulating universal propositions, pursuing graces and salvation, and promoting social unity. My informants were well aware that differences in religious belief and behavior have the potential to factionalize and antagonize, yet significantly they categorized this divisiveness as external to religion. It is *fazendo politica na religião* (mixing politics into religion). It is politics which is by definition conflictual. When asked to define and describe *politica,* informants repeatedly used words like divisive, particularistic, aggressive, dangerous, and destructive. It was unanimously agreed that a concern with politics interfered with one's religious mission and would almost certainly impair chances for attaining salvation. It would appear that the messiah, Pedro Batista, was criticized for using his god-given knowledge and talents (by definition, all-encompassing and universalistic) for particularistic and potentially divisive ends. He is said, for example, to have seriously endangered the community by having courted rival politicians. One of these threatened to destroy the community by force if he did not receive the majority of its votes.

What implications for political action can be drawn from this cultural categorization? The legacy of the Portuguese remains. A marked separation exists between religion and politics. Many Northeasterners persist in the belief that only the former should be the concern of the poor. It is perhaps a significant observation that among populations like the Melanesians and American Indians where politics and religion were not discrete categories of meaning and action, more politically oriented movements resulted than in Northeast Brazil, where these domains are discrete and opposed. In the case of Northeast Brazil, a set of meanings and orientations which possess the potential for reconstituting power relations has not been realized. The political potential for millenarianism for the oppressed has been subordinated to a rigid subdivision and hierarchy between religion and politics.

RELIGION AND THE POLITICAL ECONOMY OF THE NORTHEAST

Having explored the cultural constraints upon the politicization of Brazilian millenarian movements, I do not want to convey the impression that I believe the sole determinant is cultural. Earlier it was argued that the salvationist world view of the poor was derived from an ideology created by the Portuguese conquerors. Whatever were the initial motivations of the Portuguese, over time their beliefs came to legitimate their own domination and to accustom the poor to seek rewards outside of society. As in the past, so in the present, the salvationist tradition and the accommodational nature of folk Catholicism must be understood in relationship to the political and economic relations which condition and sustain the beliefs and religious orientations.

In pursuing this line of argument, I want to stress that the acceptance of religious teachings that has long legitimated inequality and fostered accommodation to the politicoeconomic system has not reflected political naïveté. The paucity of peasant rebellion in the Northeast indicates that the poor have assessed their interests as being better served by accommodation than rebellion.

As studies of peasant social movements have documented (Wolf 1969; Migdal 1974), certain conditions must be met if these are to evolve into rebellions or revolutions. These include institutions that support horizontal linkages among the poor, control over sufficient land, food, and weapons to sustain a peasant army, and leaders who are knowledgeable about regional and national political institutions. The Brazilian peasantry have never had these advantages. In recognizing this situation, we may better appreciate the peasants' emphasis on millenarianism as being religious, rather than political.

For millenarian movements to have assumed an aggressive and violent orientation (i.e., *politica*), the followers would have had to have more political and economic resources or a greater appreciation for the worsening and inescapability of their spiritual and material plight.[10] By affirming in word and action to themselves and to those in power that their orientation was religious, the poor were actually at times able to improve their spiritual and material condition. If they had adopted a political orientation, the followers would have faced far better equipped rivals, rather than patrons who recognized their worth in votes and labor and extended to them limited political and material benefits.

Perhaps the majority of millenarianists did not make these logical connections between religious means and gains in spiritual and material ends. Like other Northeasterners, nonetheless, they must have recognized that with opportunities for subsistence or minor improvement available, and with all political resources in the hands of the ruling class, accepting and working within the existing politicoeconomic system represented the only feasible option available to them. Politics truly was, and continues to be, the domain of the rich. Religion provides a vehicle by which the constraints facing the poor are understood, endured, and in rare instances diminished.[11]

THE POWER OF THE WORD

If as action taken by Northeast peasants, millenarianism is best understood as being oriented by and toward religious ends, does this mean that there is no relationship between politics and millenarianism? If for the actors, millenarianism is perceived to be religious and passive, can we predict that it will be encouraged by those in power who view it as a fortuitous mechanism of social control? Millenarianism appears to have been viewed in this light during the years of the Republic and during the Populist years. From the late 1880s through to the mid-1900s, millenarian groups were attributed value by politicians. This was due to their numbers of potential electors, men who might serve in personal militias,[12] and to the movements' general accommodational nature.

This positive attribution no longer exists, and I believe it will not resurface in Brazil while an authoritarian state remains in power. At present it is the overseers of this repressive government who have determined what the operant definition of millenarianism will be, and it is a meaning very different from that held by would-be millenarianists.

A lesson may be learned from this fact. There is a tendency among symbolists either to view divergent meanings as meeting equally within symbolic interaction (a kind of democracy of symbolic action) or to assume that symbols are shared or are more or less consensually understood (Mead 1934; Geertz 1973). Experience and observation demonstrate, nonetheless, that democracy or consensus in meaning does not operate in many social situations. One of the ways leaders and elites gain and maintain power is by assuming the advantage in defining phenomena and convincing or coercing others to act with reference to their definition (Edelman 1964, 1971). In addressing ourselves to this social process, we begin to explore the crucial link between symbols and power. The meanings associated with millenarianism and the functions millenarianism assumed have articulated and continue to articulate with the political needs and constraints of those seeking power during different phases of Brazilian history.

With the establishment of a military dictatorship in 1964, power was centralized, elections were controlled by the state, and urban and rural unions were prohibited. In this authoritarian political environment, social movements not directly linked to the government's ideology and interests have come to be looked upon by national and local politicians as potentially subversive and best disbanded at the start. This response can be traced to the government's recognition that it does not have broad-based popular support. Leaders fear that expressions of dissent can easily spread, especially in geographically remote and poor regions like the Northeast. Defined in the category of the potentially subversive, millenarian activities are scrutinized and controlled. The poor of the millenarian community of Santa Brigida, for example, have met with failure each time they have attempted to establish a new messiah in the place of their recently deceased leader. The local politicians, working in conjunction with the locally based military, have prevented the man from settling, by threatening the messianic figure and his followers with legal prosecution. This political pressure has effectively impeded the creation of a new millenarian movement among the poor in Santa Brigida.

Worsley (1957) and Hobsbawm (1959) have argued that millenarian movements will disappear as individuals learn to express their needs and demands in political rather than religious terms. There are two assumptions behind this belief. The first is that millenarianism is, at root, a political phenomenon. The second is that religious expressions are examples of false consciousness and will be replaced by more appropriate and realistic political ones.

While I agree in part with Worsley and Hobsbawm's conclusions, I must point to another cause for the decline of activist millenarian movements. Rather than by a "maturing consciousness," the decline of activist millenarian movements around the world will be determined by a "maturing state." The majority of millenarian movements have occurred either during periods of little political centralization and control, or during periods when the movements were used for political gain within a fluid and competitive political system. It appears that with a trend toward the consolidation of power, modern states are increasingly coopting, suppressing, or rendering peripheral popular movements that possess antagonistic or idiosyncratic ideologies and orientations. In a political system like that of the United States in which politicians perceive themselves to have popular support, millenarian activities can be tolerated in religious cults like the Peyote Church, the Black Muslims, and the cult of Reverend Moon. Nonetheless, these activities are carefully scrutinized for signs of political orientation and volatility. If these should appear, legal action is taken against the cult members. In a political regime like that currently in power in Brazil, the degree of flexibility found in the United States is perceived to be too risky. Millenarianism is defined as political and antagonistic to the interests of the state.

I disagree with the contention that millenarianism will disappear with a transformation in mentality. As illustrated by the thwarted attempt to establish a new messiah in Santa Brigida, and as reflected in instances of Americans' conversions to evangelical and Eastern millenial faiths, concern for salvation and heaven on earth are dead neither in Brazil nor the United States. Concern with inequality, suffering, and death will presumably always be present. Furthermore, in the case of Northeast Brazil the widening socioeconomic gulf between rich and poor and the increasing loss of land by the peasants should provide as suitable a context for millenarian explanations and orientations as such dislocation did in the past.

It is the power of the state and its monopoly on meaning, not the potential revolutionary symbols and properties nor the religious and accommodating nature of millenarian beliefs, that has captured the day. This marked suppression of the people's interests and aspirations, however, cannot be sustained indefinitely. A set of questions arises. Will millenarianism reemerge in its role of accommodating people to the present, while in pursuit of divine salvation? Will the processes of religious secularization,[13] of alienation of the poor from their land, and of the creation of large-scale underemployment combine to overcome the moderating role of religion over politics? Will Northeasterners be able to overcome the constraints imposed by the state, so as to forge a militant peasant movement that may be guided in part by millennial symbols and goals? These remain questions that a symbolic approach allows one to pose; a symbolic analysis is not precise enough to allow for the prediction of which of these possible alternatives may be realized once the military dictatorship is dismantled.

NOTES

1. The material upon which this paper is based was collected during two field trips to Northeast Brazil, August 1973–November 1974 and June–August 1977. The first period of research was supported by grants from the Doherty Foundation and the National Institute of Mental Health. I would like to thank the many Northeasterners who so graciously allowed me to observe and participate in their lives. I also wish to thank Jan Brukman and Gil Joseph for their comments on an earlier draft of this paper.

2. Weber argued that modifications in economic and social institutions were necessary conditions for the rise of capitalism, but he viewed Calvinism as the enabling force behind the first capitalist societies.

3. Geertz argues that modifications in one system will not necessarily be reflected in the other, since the social and cultural systems are based upon different organizing principles. He contrasts the "causal-functional integration" of the social system to the "logico-meaningful integration" of the cultural system (Geertz 1973: 145).

4. I understand millenarianism to be a set of meanings which illustrate how paradise or heaven on earth can be imminently attained through the reversal of the present order. Commonly the climactic moment is to be brought about by supernatural agents who recognize the worthiness of the millenarianists' actions.

5. For another discussion of the dramatic nature of millenarian ideologies, see Talmon 1965.

6. The terms selected to demonstrate the dramatic structure of millenarian ideologies are appropriate for an ideology from a Judeo-Christian tradition. The conceptual units appropriate to an ideology unrelated to this tradition would be different but could be equally accommodated to the dramatic pentad.

7. Worsley's diachronic study of cargo cults in Melanesia reveals that symbolic manipulation may not only help to raise political consciousness but may also assist in the creation of new and more viable political institutions. In the initial Melanesian movements, the nature of the colonial experience as understood by the Europeans was captured symbolically by the millenarianists. Europeans and natives were opposed as good and evil, knowledgeable and ignorant, overseers and laborers. A just and appropriate resolution was envisioned of these values and relationships the Europeans had defined and enforced. The natives were to regain their rightful control over decision making, resources, and labor. The Europeans were to become the victims of their own injustice, assuming the dehumanizing role they had created for the natives. Worsley's findings suggest that the final movements assumed a clearly political and rational form because the earlier acts of distortion, inversion, and rejection allowed the Melanesians to question the validity and utility not only of colonial relationships and institutions but of traditional ones as well. The latter, he argues, were unsuited to the European, bureaucratized political system which the Melanesians had to confront in order to gain self-representation and independence.

8. The missionary Antonio Vieira claimed: "The Portuguese reign was founded on July 25, 1139, when Dom Afonso I. Henriques conquered the Moors in Turkey. God had said to the King at the dawn of this victory: 'I want you and your descendants to establish my kingdom' (The words of God to Gideon in the Old Testament). . . . All the Kings are of God, but the other kings are God's, produced by men; the king of Portugal is of God and Created by God, and thus more rightly His" (Hoornaert 1974: 35).

9. This position is summarized in a seventeenth-century sermon delivered to the slaves and tenants on a large Northeast sugar plantation:

There is not a type of work nor way of life more similar to the Cross and Passion of Christ than yours on these plantations. Fortunate are you who recognize the gift of your state, how conformity to and imitation of such a high and divine resemblance enhances and sanctifies the work! On a plantation you are imitators of the crucified Christ, because you suffer in a manner very similar to the Lord who suffered on His Cross, in all His Passion. His Cross was composed of two slats, and yours on the plantation is composed of three. And there, as well, cane was not lacking, because it entered twice during the Passion. . . . Part of the Passion of Christ consisted of a night without sleep, and part of a day without rest, such are your days and nights. Christ despised and you despised; Christ without food, and you knowing hunger; Christ in every way maltreated, and you in every way maltreated. The shackles, the prisons, the whips, the wounds, the curses, of all this is your imitation composed, and if it is accompanied with patience so it too will possess the merit of martyrdom. (Hoornaert 1974: 86)

10. When severe economic reversals have struck the Northeast other regions have experienced booms. Thus migrants from the Northeast have been able to secure temporary or permanent employment elsewhere. Faco (1972) argues that during the crisis of the late 1800s and early 1900s, employment in the North and Southeast alleviated the violent pressure that a numerous population entirely deprived of basic subsistence might have come to exercise over the estate system.

11. I have argued that to understand more fully the accommodational role of religious meanings and beliefs these must be placed in the context of the Northeast political economy. Two examples of the use of religious symbols for political ends further illustrate this point. Both examples involve the use of religious symbols within political settings. Given the context of the political action, only the second represents the use of religious symbols in a manner congruent with the peasants' interests.

Millenarian communities like Joaseiro and Canudos have participated in "Holy Wars" in which religious symbols have played an important part. It must be emphasized, however, that these battles did not grow out of the ideology of the movements. They were imposed on them from the outside. To protect their religious communities, millenarianists were forced to fight for the interests of their patron—a member of the ruling class—not for their own political and material interests.

A counter-example of how religious meanings may be used to further peasants' political interests is found in the Peasant Leagues of the 1960s. In this case, peasants were able to link up with and gain support from national political movements. Here we find religious symbols employed by peasant leaders to expose the immorality of the peasants' subordination to landlords, politicians, and merchants. This latter example illustrates that, given the proper context, skillfully chosen and elaborated religious symbols may contribute to political action on the part of the peasantry.

Why religion finally emerged in the 1960s from its accommodational role is a most provocative question. Following the arguments made in the body of the paper, I would suggest that one factor was the change in the peasants' assessment of the viability of active protest. With transformations having occurred in national and local politics, Northeast peasants were willing to take a risk and looked to their religion for legitimation and emotional support. Another factor was that educated rural and urban leaders were able to make the synthesis between religion, self-liberation, and political liberation. For example, peasants were introduced, perhaps for the first time, to Christ the rebel.

12. See Della Cava (1968) for a discussion of how the political chiefs coopted millenarian movements by exchanging a promise of protection for labor and votes.

13. Another change in religion may alter its predominant role in encouraging accommodation to the existing sociocultural system. I refer to the commitment of many members of the Latin American church to transform

ecclesiastical institutions and teachings into forces for social change and liberation. Unfortunately, since the revolution of 1964, the most committed clergy in Brazil have been effectively prevented from working toward these goals.

My experience with peasants in the Northeast has convinced me that a fatalistic and penitential Catholicism can only be modified by demonstrating to this population that liberation Catholicism has its roots both in the Bible and in society. The latter must provide Norheasterners with sufficient opportunities to challenge the popular belief that "God choses one's fate at birth, and to be born with a planet to be poor is to be closer to God and more likely to receive salvation."

REFERENCES

Aberle, David, 1962. A Note on Relative Deprivation Theory as Applied to Millenarian and Other Cult Movements. In *Millennial Dreams in Action,* Sylvia Trupp, ed. (The Hague: Mouton and Company), pp. 552–57.

Cohn, Norman, 1961. *The Pursuit of the Millennium* (New York: Oxford University Press).

da Cunha, Euclides, 1944. *Rebellion in the Backlands* (Chicago: University of Chicago Press).

Della Cava, Ralph, 1968. Brazillian Messianism and National Institutions: A Review of Canudos and Joaseiro. *Hispanic American Review* 48(3): 402–20.

———, 1970. *Miracle at Joaseiro* (New York: Columbia University Press).

Douglas, Mary, 1966. *Purity and Danger* (London: Routledge and Kegan Paul).

Edelman, Murray, 1964. *The Symbolic Uses of Politics* (Urbana: University of Illinois Press).

———, 1971. *Politics as Symbolic Action* (Chicago: Markham).

Faco, Rui, 1972. *Cangaceiros e Fanaticos* (Rio de Janeiro: Editora Civilização Brasileira).

Firth, Raymond, 1973. *Symbols* (Ithaca, N.Y.: Cornell University Press).

Geertz, Clifford, 1973. *Interpretations of Culture* (New York: Basic Books).

Gonçalves Couto, Padre Manoel Jose, 1873. *Missão Abreviada* (Porto, Portugal).

Hobsbawm, E. J., 1959. *Primitive Rebels* (Manchester, England: Manchester University Press).

Hoornaert, Edwardo, 1974. *Formação do Catolicismo Brasileiro: 1550–1800* (Petropolis: Editora Vozes).

Lanternari, Vittorio, 1963. *The Religions of the Oppressed* (London: MacGibbon and Kee).

Lawrence, Peter, 1964. *Road Belong Cargo* (Manchester, England: Manchester University Press).

Mead, George Herbert, 1934. *Mind, Self, and Society* (Chicago: University of Chicago Press).

Migdal, Joel, 1974. *Peasants, Politics, and Revolution* (Princeton: Princeton University Press).

Perieira de Queiroz, Maria, 1965. *O Messianismo no Brasil e no Mundo* (São Paulo: Editora de Universidade São Paulo).
Talmon, Yonina, 1965. Pursuit of the Millennium: The Relation between Religious and Social Change. In *Reader in Comparative Religion*, William Lessa and Evon Vogt, eds. (New York: Harper and Row), pp. 209–14.
Turner, Victor, 1967. *The Forest of Symbols* (Ithaca, N.Y.: Cornell University Press).
————, 1974. *Dramas, Fields, and Metaphors* (Ithaca, N.Y.: Cornell University Press).
Wallace, Anthony, 1961. *Culture and Personality* (New York: Random House).
Weber, Max, 1947. *Theory of Social and Economic Organization* (New York: Free Press).
Wolf, Eric, 1969. *Peasant Wars of the Twentieth Century* (New York: Harper and Row).
Worsley, Peter, 1957. *The Trumpet Shall Sound* (London: MacGibbon and Kee).

Shonto in 1989:
A Culture Historian Looks at the Future

WILLIAM Y. ADAMS

   This study focuses on a group of Navajo families inhabiting an up-land district of canyons and mesas, about thirty miles long and fifteen miles wide, in the remote and sparsely settled northwestern quarter of the Navajo Indian Reservation. Although designated for convenience as the Shonto Community, these families do not constitute a community in the accepted sense of the term, for they are widely dispersed in extended family settlements throughout the whole of the district. They are set apart from other Navajo families in surrounding areas only in that they do most of their shopping at Shonto Trading Post, send their children to Shonto Community School, and have since 1956 been members of the Shonto chapter of the Navajo tribal organization. The trading post, school, and chapter house are all located at a common point near the middle of the district, but there is otherwise no significant concentration of population in this particular vicinity.

   The Navajo families at Shonto were the subjects of an intensive social and economic study between 1954 and 1956 (Adams 1963) and of a second study in 1971 (Ruffing 1972; Adams and Ruffing 1977). During the seventeen-year interval between the two studies, some fairly dramatic material changes took place. Paved roads, which in 1954 did not pass within seventy miles of Shonto, were extended to and through the district, and nearly every family exchanged the familiar and traditional wagon for a pickup truck. The much-publicized Black Mesa coal mines began operating at the southern extremity of the area, and to serve the needs of the miners a small new town grew up nearby. An electric railroad was built to haul the Black Mesa coal to a power plant on Lake Powell. The Navajo tribal organization, temporarily enriched by production royalties from oil and mining, for the first time became a significant factor in the lives of Shonto Navajos by distributing a part of its income in the form of construction and employment projects and welfare.

   Material changes between 1954 and 1971 were not paralleled by comparable changes in the social and economic spheres, in spite of a

61 percent increase in the community's population (from 568 to 913 individuals, and from 100 to 131 households). Nevertheless, Shonto had been and remained one of the most conservative areas on the Navajo reservation, adhering to the extended family basis of social and economic organization and continuing to value the traditional economic pursuits of sheep raising and agriculture above much more remunerative wage work. The most significant changes that could be observed between the first and second studies involved a shift in dependence from off-reservation to on-reservation wage work and a threefold increase in the level of welfare payments of one form and another. Although the proportion of income derived from traditional pursuits of agriculture, animal husbandry, native medicine, and weaving diminished by half, from 26 percent to 13 percent, there was still a tendency to give top priority to these activities and to regard all forms of cash income as secondary.

At the conclusion of the original study I had expected and stated that material advancement and modernization would bring about more breakdown in the traditional social and economic order than actually took place (Adams 1963: 94). The results obtained by the 1971 restudy were considerably at variance with expectations. That experience should serve as a caution regarding the value of any prediction I might now offer. With some trepidation I will nevertheless suggest some possibilities as to what Shonto might be like after another seventeen-year interval; that is to say, in 1989.

My predictions must necessarily apply to the future of Shonto community as a collectivity rather than to its members as individuals. A good many Shonto Navajos will unquestionably emigrate from the area and will work out their individual destinies in the mainstream of American life with varying degrees of success or failure. Some will perhaps return in triumph and some in defeat to the ancestral community; many probably never will return. My concern must, however, be restricted to those families who choose to remain at least partially integrated within the Shonto interaction sphere.

SCENARIOS FOR THE FUTURE

Since completing the initial study of Shonto in 1956 I have been engaged almost entirely in culture-historical investigations, which means that I have become much more accustomed to retrodicting than to predicting culture change. My task has been to deduce the processes of change leading up to a given result, rather than vice versa. Through this experience I have been made aware of a number of different and to some extent opposed models for the explanation of change, for the debate over alternative theories has come very much to the fore among culture historians in the recent past. Unlike some of my colleagues, however, I have never been very satisfied with monistic approaches; I have found that the complex realities of history and prehistory are best understood by considering and combining the results obtained from several different explanatory models (see Adams 1977: 665–80). I hope therefore that I may be forgiven for bringing the same eclecticism to bear in considering the future of Shonto. I should like to begin by viewing the community's future from a number of different theoretical perspectives and to reserve judgment among them until later. I will consider theories derived partly from the literature of culture history and partly from applied anthropology, beginning with the most specific and ascending toward the most general.

Linear projection. Shonto is one of a very small number of communities that have been intensively studied not once but twice, so that the extent of culture change between two points in time can not only be described but can also be measured (Adams and Ruffing 1977). With that kind of baseline data, the simplest kind of prediction would foresee nothing more than a continuation of the trends defined by the earlier studies. In this scenario there would be a steady increase in the adoption of American material goods and comforts by the Shonto Navajos, including such things as American-style houses, furniture, and appliances (presuming that electricity becomes available within the area). Shonto's total population would undergo a further increase from 913 to 1470 individuals and from 131 to 172 households, but traditional social organization by nuclear and extended family groups would not be affected. There would be a slight increase in the number of emigrants from the community and in dependence on wage work in place of traditional farming and animal husbandry, but the latter pursuits would continue to be most valued by Shonto Navajos. Dependence on welfare payments would continue to rise proportionately with the community's population, since no significant increase in job opportunities can be forecast. The persistence of traditional social organization and values would be mirrored by continuing adherence to Navajo religious beliefs and practices, even though increasing numbers would also formally enroll as Christians at the newly established Shonto Mission.

Linear projection models are often employed by economists and demographers for short-range prediction; they are also employed for retrodiction by culture historians. They have seldom been popular with applied anthropologists, perhaps because applied anthropologists usually do not like what they see happening to the world's native and peasant peoples, and therefore prefer to hope that it will not continue.

In the case of Shonto, the unexpected conservatism and cultural persistence revealed by the 1971 restudy suggest that linear projection might actually be the safest model for predicting the community's future in 1989, but the same would assuredly not be true for the year 2089. A continued linear increase in population will before long reduce the average range holding per family to the point where sheep raising will no longer be possible. Once this traditional agrarian basis is removed, it is doubtful that the corporate integrity of the extended family group will survive. Moreover, there is probably a limit to the ability and willingness either of American taxpayers or of the Navajo tribe to support the increases in Shonto's population with proportional increases in unemployment and welfare payments. I therefore suggest that the present tradition-based socio-economic order might last another seventeen years, but its days are numbered.

Parallel case study. Another key to Shonto's future might be found in the study of Navajo communities that have been exposed for a longer time to the interpenetration of American economic, material, and educational influences—i.e., to the same forces that may now be seen at work at Shonto. Most such communities are located on the eastern side of the Navajo reservation, an area where population density has also reached a much higher figure than is currently found at Shonto (Kunitz 1977: 188).

A number of eastern Navajo communities have been the subject of studies in the past twenty-five years (Henderson and Levy 1975: 37–83); of these probably the fullest data come from Fruitland (Sasaki 1960). If it is to serve as a paradigm for the future of Shonto, then we shall have to envision a breakdown of the traditional social order and the replacement of the extended family by the nuclear family as the basic residential and corporate unit. This will be accompanied by a shift away from matrilocal and to a lesser extent away from patrilocal residence patterns and toward the establishment of neolocal residences in areas close to available sources of wage work. Many families will give up sheep raising altogether. There will be a decline in the appeal and in the prestige of traditional Navajo religion, but it will not be offset by a rush to embrace other ideologies. On the contrary, the erosion of traditional beliefs and values will be accompanied by demoralization, anomie, an increase in interpersonal tensions and conflict, and an exacerbation of the community's already considerable problems with alcohol.

This rather dismal prognosis is probably also a fairly realistic one.

Nevertheless, recent studies have suggested that there may be structural differences in the society and economy of eastern and western Navajo groups that are not merely the result of differential acculturation (Aberle 1961; Kunitz 1977). If so, Fruitland and other eastern communities do not necessarily offer a wholly accurate paradigm for the future of Shonto and other western areas.

An acculturation/assimilation model. From about 1880 to 1930, and intermittently in subsequent years, it was the intention and policy of the United States government that Indians should be culturally and socially integrated into the mainstream of American life and should lose their separate identity and status. This ideal was inspired by the apparently successful assimilation of European immigrants. It was wholeheartedly endorsed not merely by the Indian Bureau but by the great majority of social activists and reformers and by Indian leaders themselves. There were times when it seemed that the only voices raised against Indian assimilation were those of anthropologists (who, it must be acknowledged, had a vested interest in the preservation of separate Indian cultures and communities). Assimilation was nevertheless one of the possible outcomes of culture contact acknowledged in the "acculturation studies" that became popular in the middle years of this century (Linton 1940: 464; Spicer 1961: 531–32).

An acculturation/assimilation model would assume that under the pressures and conditions of culture contact Navajos would become increasingly "American" in each generation until little or nothing of the aboriginal culture survived, and the label "Navajo" would cease to have any meaning. This has happened over and over again to ethnic minorities in other times and places, and some current developments at Shonto seem to point in the same direction. Between 1954 and 1971, for example, the average number of school years completed by Shonto youth increased from about three to more than ten, and this surely implies an increase in knowledge at least of the content of modern American culture. Simultaneously there has been a decrease in knowledge of the traditional content of Navajo culture—not only of myth and ritual, but also of much of its arcane technology. A linear and indefinite projection of this process would end in the complete replacement of Navajo by American culture traits, as indeed really happened with many European immigrant groups. The process of course would be far from complete by 1989.

As a paradigm for the eventual assimilation of the Shonto Navajos we may look not to other Navajo communities but to other Indian tribes with a longer history of culture contact. Some tribes have of course disappeared from the map through total extermination, but others have disappeared because all of their members have made the transition from Indians to modern Americans. We have to recognize, however, that acculturation does not necessarily and automatically lead to assimilation. Acculturation may often be a collective experience, but in America assimilation must always be an individual one. Individual Indians continually pass into the American mainstream and cease to be Indians, but no tribe has ever been collectively incorporated. On the contrary, in the Dakotas and Oklahoma we see examples of tribes whose cultural transformation into Americans is virtually complete but who continue to maintain ethnic boundaries and identity precisely because there is no place for them as collectivities in American society.

Since assimilation is mainly an individual affair, the most effective way to compel the assimilation of Navajos and other Indians would be to break up the reservations (as was actually done with many Plains reservations in the 1880s); the surest way to forestall assimilation would be to preserve the reservations intact. As I will suggest later, either of these things could happen, for reasons that are outside the control of the Navajos themselves.

A pluralistic/configurationist model. The term "incorporation" was introduced into the ethnographic literature by Evon Vogt to describe the pattern of Navajo response to culture contact (Vogt 1961: 328). It is seen as the conceptual antithesis of assimilation. "The essence of this process is that elements from other cultures are incorporated into Navajo culture in such a way that the structural framework of the institutional core . . . is maintained, and the borrowed elements are fitted into place and elaborated in terms of the pre-existing patterns" (Vogt 1961: 328). Vogt elsewhere asserts that "it is . . . clear that *cultural content,* or the cultural inventory, has undergone impressive changes since about 1700, but insofar as I can determine, the structural framework of this institutional core has persisted with remarkable continuity" (Vogt 1961: 327). The same point of view has been strongly expressed by Kluckhohn and Leighton (1942; 1946) and many other writers. Essentially this is the configurationist outlook, a temporarily powerful intellectual current in anthropology which sprung from the inspiration of Benedict and Kroeber.

The overall lack of change at Shonto since 1954 would seem to give cogency to the configurationist point of view. Indeed, I myself have argued in another place that the relative success of Navajos in maintaining a viable separate identity through all kinds of historical vicissitudes has been due to their nimbleness in adapting material and economic innovations in such a way that their most cherished social values are not threatened (Adams 1971). I am nevertheless pessimistic as to how much longer this can continue. For all its demonstrated resilience, the core of Navajo culture cannot be infinitely malleable. For that reason I am certain that the day will come when it will give way. It may hold until 1989, but almost certainly not until 2089.

A neoevolutionist model. Among culture historians currently the most fashionable explanatory model is the neoevolutionist or cultural materialist model, which derives ultimately from Karl Marx. According to neoevolutionists, all significant and patterned culture change proceeds ultimately from environmental causes. Human groups cope with their environment through technology, which in turn shapes social and ideological institutions to fit. The neoevolutionists have not yet gone very far in applying their model to the constraints of human as opposed to natural environments, but it is clear at least by implication that the exploitation of humans comes to replace the exploitation of nature as the basic adaptive strategy of advancing societies. Increasing inequalities of political and economic power lead to the formation of proletariats, whose coerced productivity then becomes the basic resource on which states and empires are built.

The neoevolutionists, perhaps reflecting the persisting influence of Marx, have been much more forthright on the subject of historical inevitability than have other students of culture change. If, as they devoutly believe, they have discovered an immutable historical law, then it will surely not be suspended in favor of the Navajos. They will be dispossessed and exploited like all the world's other subjugated and colonized peoples as long as any profit can be derived from them and in the end will be left resourceless to work out their destinies in any way they can.

Up to a point one can find support for the neoevolutionist position in the situation of Navajos who have temporarily or permanently left the reservation and who can find no niche in modern American society except at the lowest levels of the urban proletariat (McCracken 1968; Graves 1970). Yet it is not economically clear why the American system tolerates the perpetuation of the Navajo Reservation, which somewhat artificially protects the majority of Navajos from making the transition from tribesmen to proletarians. Whatever the public outcry might be, it is well within the power of the government to abrogate the Treaty of 1868; after all, it has already outlived more than 99 percent of all international treaties.

Studies of culture change in other areas have demonstrated to my satisfaction that the would-be laws of the neoevolutionists have something less than total explanatory power, and I therefore have limited faith in their ability to predict the future of Shonto either in the short or in the long run.

An idealist model. As a longtime reader of *Human Organization,* I am aware that the majority of applied anthropologists are, as I believe they properly should be, idealists. In the prediction of culture change they may in consequence be ruled more by their hearts than by their heads. A typical applied anthropologist's vision of the future, I suspect, would begin with a choice of the most desirable of possible outcomes in any given contact situation and would then construct a scenario through which desired outcome *could* be achieved. Anthropologists being what they are, the desired outcome would almost certainly involve the perpetuation of cultural and ethnic differences, and the scenario to achieve it would require overt government or public intervention to forestall the normal processes of cultural destruction. Applied to the Navajos, such a model would be realistic in its recognition that the future of American Indians will be determined much more by the general direction of American social policy than by anything the Indians themselves may do. It would be unrealistic, however, in assuming that social policy will be much influenced by the advice of anthropologists.

It is nevertheless true for the moment that the main ideas of social philosophy in this country are more nearly in tune with the thinking of anthropologists than they have ever been in the past. This is reflected in environmental and conservation policies as well as in our new-found tolerance for cultural and ethnic differences. As long as the rapport lasts there is always some hope that the dreams of anthropologists may find fulfillment through national policies.

The Uncertain Winds of Ideology. I would be false to my deepest intellectual convictions if I professed much faith in any of the predictive models I have just been discussing, or in any others. I have elsewhere asserted (Adams 1977: 673–78) and will here reiterate my belief that the stylistic as opposed to the goal-related element in culture is very significant and that it is not susceptible to rationalistic, maximization models of explanation. Many things change for the better, and many things change under compulsion, but many things also change simply because we grow tired of constancy and repetition. This fundamental reality applies no less at the level of ideology and policy than at that of dress and decoration. At the present time, for example, we seem to be warming toward the Chinese simply because we are tired of hating them and cooling toward Israel for the opposite reason.

No one is more at the mercy of the shifting winds of ideology than the American Indian. It has been the peculiar fate of the Indian to become, for the great majority of us, a symbol and metaphor for qualities in our national character and our national experience that we intermittently cherish and yearn to revive. For better or worse, the Indian's destiny is more bound up in that symbolic identity than in the practical realities of economics.

For a hundred years and more official policy toward the Indian has shifted uncertainly between the ideals of assimilation and of cultural pluralism, often in response to factors having little to do with the Indians themselves. The "treaty era" immediately following the wars of pacification saw an unquestioning acceptance of the principle of Indian separatism, even at the price of supporting a whole generation of Indians on rations. This highly paternalistic treatment was probably prompted by the feelings of guilt engendered by the barbarities of the Indian wars themselves. The initial sense of guilt, however, was soon submerged beneath a wave of smug national self-satisfaction and a social Darwinist philosophy, which found expression in "the white man's burden" and "manifest destiny." The American sense of cultural superiority, in particular, was reinforced by the experience of successfully absorbing and integrating millions of European immigrants. Not surprisingly, in that climate of limitless optimism, Americans came to feel that the greatest gift they could bestow on the red man was the privilege of entering as rapidly as possible into the American mainstream and shedding tribal identity. This was to be accomplished through the termination of rations and where appropriate through the breaking up of the reservations into individually owned parcels, under the Dawes Act of 1887. As a result of its application, many Plains tribes lost more than two-thirds of their land within a generation. Southwestern tribes were spared a similar fate only because their territorial rights were in some cases guaranteed by our treaty with Mexico in 1848.

In the early 1900s idealistic assimilationism subsided into benign neglect, as it became apparent that America's destiny was to be an urban-industrial and not an agrarian nation. Social consciousness came to focus increasingly on the problems of Eastern cities rather than on rural peoples, either Indian or white. Assimilation nevertheless remained the official goal both of our Indian and of our immigration policy, though after 1900 Asiatics were excluded from this ideal. Meanwhile flagging national self-confidence was revitalized by the jingo patriotism of World War I and the prolonged prosperity that followed it.

The crash of 1929 and the depression that followed unleashed a wave both of proletarianism and of back-to-the-soil Rousseauian idealism, both of which conspicuously benefited the American Indian as the symbolic exemplar of newly rediscovered virtues. The Collier regime in the Bureau of Indian Affairs, heavily influenced by anthropologists, made cultural pluralism once again the official policy of the bureau. The alienation of Indian lands was not only halted but reversed, Indians were given the right of self-government within limits, restrictions on the practice of native religion were relaxed, and federal money was made available for all kinds of reservation development. On the Navajo Reservation the socially disruptive effects of the boarding school system were mitigated by the construction of a network of local day schools all over the reservation.

The halcyon days of revived sympathy for a separate Indian destiny lasted only a decade, when the intervention of World War II brought a fresh wave of jingo nationalism. It was maintained for many years afterward by the "holy crusade" against Communism, which kept our sense of national superiority and national destiny fanned to an unnaturally high pitch. In that climate there was once again, inevitably, a strong sentiment to terminate all special treatment of the Indian and let him "sink or swim like the rest of us." The move toward termination was defeated not so much by public opinion as by the Indians' increasingly successful recourse to the courts, where they demanded proper compliance with the terms of their respective treaties.

The most recent ideological paroxysm to affect the Indians is of course the Viet Nam War, the aftereffects of which are still very much in evidence. The Viet Nam generation forced upon us a new tolerance for alien cultures and other ways of life, rooted this time in a deep American self-loathing. A small army of hippies and drop-outs gave expression to what was for a time a widespread sentiment: repudiating American materialism in favor of a way of life supposedly modelled on that of the aboriginal American. Although this sentiment appears gradually to be receding, we are still far from a return to national self-confidence, and the Indian continues to benefit from our misgivings. For example, a recent policy decision makes all Navajos eligible for relief who cannot find a job within reasonable commuting distance of their place of residence—a category which includes virtually the entire adult population at Shonto (Adams and Ruffing 1977: 80). This represents an assumption of economic responsibility on the part of government that would have been unthinkable a generation ago and one which is still not applied to non-Indians. Put into full practice, it would constitute nothing less than a revival of the rations systems of a hundred years ago—a subsidy paid to Indians to encourage them to stay on the reservation.

Given the increasing trend toward industrialization and capitalization in every sector of the American economy, the prospects for Indian economic self-sufficiency are virtually nil. This means quite simply that their ability to maintain a separate cultural and social identity depends in the end on our willingness to subsidize them when they do so. For the time being, as I have indicated, that willingness is high—perhaps higher than at any time in the last ninety years. But how long it will last no one can say. Up to now the pendulum swings of ideology and policy have always stopped short of the ultimate extremes of total segregation and of forced assimilation, but there is no guarantee that they always will. I can only be certain that, whatever the future holds for Shonto, it will be determined less by the Navajos than by middle-class Americans like you and me. Thus my reluctance to predict the community's future stems less from uncertainty about the Navajos than from uncertainty about where we ourselves are going.

REFERENCES

Aberle, David F., 1961. Navaho. In *Matrilineal Kinship,* David M. Schneider and Kathleen Gough, eds. (Berkeley: University of California Press), pp. 96–201.

Adams, William Y., 1963. *Shonto: A Study of the Role of the Trader in a Modern Navaho Community, Bureau of American Ethnology Bulletin 188* (Washington, D.C.: Government Printing Office).

———, 1971. Navajo Ecology and Economy: A Problem in Cultural Values. In *Apachean Culture History and Ethnology,* Keith H. Basso and Morris E. Opler, eds. (Tucson: Anthropological Papers of the University of Arizona, No. 21), pp. 77–82.

———, 1977. *Nubia: Corridor to Africa.* (London: Allen Lane).

Adams, William Y., and Lorraine T. Ruffing, 1977. Shonto Revisited: Measures of Social and Economic Change in a Navajo Community, 1956–1971. *American Anthropologist* 79: 58–83.

Graves, Theodore D., 1970. The Personal Adjustment of Navajo Indian Migrants to Denver, Colorado. *American Anthropologist* 72: 35–54.

Henderson, Eric B., and Jerrold E. Levy, 1975. *Survey of Navajo Community Studies 1936–1974.* (Los Angeles: Lake Powell Research Project Bulletin No. 6).

Kluckhohn, Clyde, 1942. The Navajos in the Machine Age. *Technology Review* 44: 2–6.

Kluckhohn, Clyde, and Dorothea Leighton, 1946. *The Navaho.* (Cambridge, Mass.: Harvard University Press).

Kunitz, Stephen J., 1977. Economic Variation on the Navajo Reservation. *Human Organization* 36: 186–93.

Linton, Ralph, ed., 1940. *Acculturation in Seven American Indian Tribes.* (New York: Appleton-Century Crofts).

McCracken, Robert D., 1968. Urban Migration and the Changing Structure of Navajo Social Relations. (Ph.D. diss., Department of Anthropology, University of Colorado).

Ruffing, Lorraine T., 1972. An Alternative Approach to Economic Development in a Traditional Navajo Community. (Ph.D. diss., Faculty of Political Science, Columbia University).

Sasaki, Tom T., 1960. *Fruitland, New Mexico: a Navaho Community in Transition.* (Ithaca, N.Y.: Cornell University Press).

Spicer, Edward H., ed., 1961. *Perspectives in American Indian Culture Change.* (Chicago: University of Chicago Press).

Vogt, Evon Z., 1961. Navaho In Edward H. Spicer, ed., *Perspectives in American Indian Culture Change* (Chicago: University of Chicago Press), pp. 278–336.

Prediction in Anthropology:
Reflections on Some Grounded Forecasts

Richard L. Henshel

I found it very pleasing and enlightening to read the chapters in this volume, originally for the Key Symposium of the Southern Anthropological Society. To develop comments on them has been quite a challenge for this sociologist. Each contribution is provocative and displays knowledge and insight into a local area. If some of my later remarks appear critical, this overall appraisal should not be forgotten. Given my background of work in social prediction (Henshel 1971, 1975a, 1975b, 1976, 1978; Henshel and Kennedy 1973), my role will be to emphasize the predictive dimension, but not to the exclusion of other aspects of interest. In reviewing a given chapter, my comments will center first on these general aspects and then move on to focus specifically on prediction. I will discuss five of the contributions singly, taking them in what seems to me to be a relevant sequence, and then conclude with more general observations.

ADAMS ON SHONTO CULTURE HISTORY

Adams proposed an eclectic approach to the problem of prediction. Using this approach, he develops "scenarios" for the future of the Shonto, using a straight-line extrapolation, a parallel evolution study of adjacent Navajo communities more "advanced" in their assimilation, an assimilation/acculturation model, a pluralist/configurationist model, a Marxian economic, technological deterministic model, and what might be called a social policy model, which he calls the "winds of ideology."

I agree with his suspicion that social policy will be the closest predictor of what the Shonto will be like in 1989; the fate of this Navajo community depends far more upon the prevailing ideology (social policy) of the United States superstructure than upon *any* internally generated dynamic within the Shonto culture, or even the relationship of Shonto with the engulfing society surrounding it. Like Adams, I place little confidence in the predictive force of any of the models of this situation—or in any eclectic synthesis. I doubt if we can predict the basic cultural changes of a community in the absence of far tighter theory (or, if you like, of real theory).

Although I found the paper interesting, it is frustrating to try to comment on it since I do not disagree with it and since it presented no concrete predictions for examination. In a sense Adams has aided his case for a lack of confidence in prediction by selecting a topic which demands prophecy (what *will* the future be like) rather than what is termed "scientific prediction" (Schuessler 1968) of the conditional form, "If *x* occurs, then *y* will follow." The latter is certainly not easily managed, but seems far more feasible than prophecy.[1]

A few comments can be made on certain features of the paper. The approach he calls "parallel case study" has an implicit requirement of a parallel evolution hypothesis, at least one writ small. This has, in its grosser forms, been condemned by generations of anthropologists. Then too, a parallel evolution hypothesis has been subjected to attack from the standpoint of economics. W. W. Rostow's *Stages of Economic Growth* notwithstanding, many economists today, especially those sympathetic to dependency theory, doubt whether second and later economic progressions take on the same characteristics as the first progression precisely because the first has already "arrived." Still, this is not to deny that insights may be obtained from such an approach provided it is not applied in dogmatic fashion, and certainly Adams is completely nondogmatic.

Adams's "pluralistic/configurationist model" posits the existence of cultural configurations (or patterns, or themes) which underlie the surface aspects of culture. Adams and, evidently, Vogt have argued that however much the superficial aspects of Navajo culture have changed over the decades, the core configurations have remained remarkably persistent. This claim ties interestingly with Harding and Clement's conception of a core "role structure" among the Ixil Maya that remains relatively fixed regardless of how much the superficial aspects of roles (their activities) may shift. The prediction in both cases is of a slower rate of change for deep structures than for surface aspects of culture.

HARDING AND CLEMENT ON ROLE STRUCTURES

Turning to study Harding and Clement's paper more closely, the above aspect—which they link to Bateson and Rappaport—is also a refinement or elaboration of configurationism. Here there are configurations, specific to a given culture, of the cognitive dimension of roles.

The approach seems to conceptualize a role as a constellation of activities which appear fixed but which actually transform themselves over historical time periods. Thus a priest today may have entirely different rights and activities from those of a priest of the eleventh century (barring ceremonial functions). Yet the myth of continuity is maintained through establishing a standard term, "priest," and a seemingly invariant role. I can think of three levels: specific activities or behaviors, activity clusters (roles), and role configurations (or role rules). The activities of each role change in response to exigencies, but the role structures remain much more constant.

I was struck by certain parallels between the paper and linguistics method and theory. In Harding and Clement's procedure, one first elicits the native understandings of roles and activities in much the same way as the linguist elicits phonemes and morphemes. Then one proposes a sort of "deep structure" of roles unrecognized by natives although used by them. This cognitive role structure should be capable of generating some of the surface rules (which activities belong with which roles), although this is not spelled out. And it is proposed that the unrecognized role structure shifts much more slowly than the visible aspects—rather like what is proposed with differing rates of change in language. One can extend this analogy too far, but insofar as it is useful it is intriguing.

The conceptualization of roles as "objects of on-going negotiation rather than static, well-defined scripts for behavior" links the authors' statement with some of the formulations of the interpretive theories in sociology, in their insistence that social structure is continuously negotiated rather than given. (See especially Hawkins and Tiedeman [1975] on the negotiation of norms.) But the insistence in the paper on the existence of a relatively fixed underlying role structure departs from the orientation. Again the similarities can easily be pushed too far but the connections are intriguing.[2]

As for the paper's predictions, the authors note that these are of two types—what I will relabel as predictions of velocity of change of role structure and predictions about specific changes in particular roles. I find the former predictions, especially the hypothesis that cognitive role structure will shift more slowly than surface activities, much more impressive and interesting. This is not to say that it presents no difficulties.

As I interpret it, the method used to obtain the "underlying dimensions" of the role structure (such as wealth, externality, and so forth) may have the same problem with labeling and naming encountered with factor analysis: a quantitative technique yields factors or dimensions with great precision, but the naming of these products is, in the final analysis, a matter of examining the constituent parts at first hand and thinking of the best overall summarizing name one can find. Naturally, at this point the technique becomes susceptible to human errors in judgment.[3] In addition, although the data in table 1 do lend support to the general prediction, the support is partial, as the authors themselves suggest, because the test is not definitive. The definitive test of the prediction will be to administer the questionnaire again in ten to twenty years.

PESSAR ON BRAZILIAN MILLENARIANISM

The paper by Pessar on millenarianism in Brazil seems an admirably competent analysis of millenarian movements in northeastern Brazil, and of the lack of other responses to existing conditions.[4] The paper serves as a reminder, in an ironic sense, of the dysfunctions for rulers of teaching exploited people the Judeo-Christian mythology of the millenium. Across a great variety of cultural contexts and historical periods the "message" of the millenium has been received in ways not intended by Christian missionaries.

But the differences within these movements are instructive too. Pessar's point that we ignore the content of millenarian movements at our peril seems well taken. To treat content as epiphenomenal and to insist that these movements are essentially political is to disregard critical differences between millenarian experiences. In contrast to the classical Judean response, to the ghost dance and the Sioux uprising, or even to the Cargo cults, the Brazilian case never amounted to political rebellion. The very symbolic content of belief which rendered the area susceptible to millenarianism also virtually precluded a leader from becoming "political."[5]

Pessar's observations about symbolists and symbolic interaction deserve amplification. She notes at one point that "democracy or consensus in meaning does not operate in many social situations. One of the ways leaders and elites gain and maintain power is by assuming the advantage in defining phenomena and convincing or coercing others to act with reference to their definition." It is intriguing that this is precisely the focus of a central debate currently underway in social problems theory between objectivist conceptions of social problems (as existing independently "out there") and subjectivist conceptions that emphasize the differential power of various groups within society to attach a social problems label to some disliked activity.[6] I refer to such works as Blumer (1971), Tallman (1976), and Manis (1976).

Admirable as the analysis is in many ways, it is, as the author notes, lamentably weak in terms of prediction. Again the comments advanced respecting Adams' paper may be emphasized: "if-then" predictions seem far more feasible than unconditional prophecies (see Henshel 1976). On the issue of where millenarian movements will appear, two sources would be very helpful, albeit in different ways. Neil Smelser's *Theory of Collective Behavior* (1963) tries to create a predictive theory of when forms of collective behavior will appear and, adopting the value-added approach from economics, attempts to specify which specific forms the collective behavior will assume. The theory is clearly not without its problems, but it is highly relevant since it is predictive (in its objective, at least) and explicitly relates to messianic millenarian movements in one of its sections. Pessar does not attempt to create a predictive theory of when millenarian movements will occur, but she does move in this direction at several points in the paper.

Another work which might be useful is Polak's *The Image of the Future* (1973, in English translation). A large portion of this book is devoted to the decline in the West of eschatological images of the future, and the significance of this decline upon the contemporary world. Millenarianism, is of course, an eschatological image par excellence. But Polak's central concern is the effect or influence of images of the future, in general, on what in fact happens in the future. His model of this is of the highest importance in understanding the influence of culture on the future.

GERLACH ON ENERGY WARS AND SOCIAL CHANGE

In Gerlach's paper on energy wars and social change, we have a careful examination of what appears to be an emerging form of protest movement, designated by the acronym SPIN. The unique advantages and defects of such a movement, with shifting coalitions and fragmented leadership, have been described and analyzed with great skill by Simmel (1923, translated 1955) and more recently by Dahrendorf (1959).[7] Relevant also are certain concepts from social psychology, particularly selective exposure and selective perception, when discussing aspects of the stability of attitudes and their resistance to propagandizing efforts. See in this regard Klapper (1960).

Some of the predictions in Gerlach's paper exhibit the delightful virtue of surprise as well as vulnerability. For instance, he relates the development of a seemingly more rational plan to reduce potential conflicts over power line siting, a plan that, though designated expressly to minimize conflict, contained built-in features that would invariably exacerbate the conflict. This was not an obvious but a surprising prediction, vulnerable to disproof by comparison with the conflicts under the older plan.

The generality of Gerlach's finding is an important topic. He has provided a prediction for the success of SPIN-type movements in some social conditions but not all. Specifically, his forecasts apply only to movements that do not interfere with the vital interests of the state as these are perceived by its decision makers. It would seem that the prognosis he presents applies only to movements perceived as permissible (even if disliked), whereas totally nonpermissible movements of the SPIN type will almost surely fail. We can think of Pessar's millenarian movements in Brazil, which are defined as a threat to the state. Perhaps Selznick's term, the "organizational weapon," best describes the radically different form of organization required in a nonpermissive environment. Gerlach appears to recognize this limitation when he notes that established orders in the United States typically escalate counter-measures so slowly that they increase rather than suppress commitment.[8]

One other appealing aspect of Gerlach's paper was his recognition of the importance of deviation-amplifying mutual causal feedback to explain an escalating confrontation in the social world. In the old days we used to call these "vicious circles," but for once a more elaborate terminology actually provides greater understanding. Maruyama's (1963) discussion of positive feedback loops may ultimately be of signal importance for an understanding of some basic social processes. The misfortune here is that sociology and anthropology first encountered feedback in terms of equilibrating systems (negative feedback, homeostasis), with *The Social System* of Parsons as the focal work. Once this model of society was successfully attacked, the entire area of cybernetics and feedback lost much of its credibility. This, I suspect, is very unfortunate because, while homeostatic mechanisms may be rare, deviation-amplifying feedback seems widespread. It was therefore gratifying to see the concept employed in explaining the escalation of power line wars.

As Gerlach notes, a problem with using the positive feedback conception is specifying the threshold for take-off.[9] Meanwhile, Nardi's paper on simulation modeling observes that "simulation models are . . . useful for ascertaining the point at which a change will 'make a difference' in a system; that is, it is a way of pinpointing a threshold effect, or the 'difference that makes a difference.' " Perhaps simulation can overcome this weakness of positive feedback if the two approaches are used in tandem.

NARDI ON THE USE OF
COMPUTER SIMULATION MODELS

The above-mentioned virtue of simulation is not the only advantage of the technique, of course, and Nardi did an excellent job of listing and describing the advantages. The disadvantages or limitations of computer simulation are also well articulated. She notes the necessity for a prior understanding of the system to be modeled, requiring a strong knowledge of the relationships between components. Knowing what can be safely omitted from the model is another vital consideration, since the model cannot reproduce every aspect yet cannot afford to leave out any component significant for the functioning of the system. (See this point especially in the discussion in Raser [1969]). Finally, the accuracy of the initial-state data is critical for some kinds of simulation—although Nardi's own does not require this, since it is about hypothetical rather than historical hunting-gathering societies.

In addition to its considerable virtues, therefore, simulation imposes rather strict requirements before its outcomes can be truly meaningful. Unfortunately, this does not preclude its misuse when the requirements have not been satisfied. The approach is not desirable for all or even most sociocultural areas at present simply because the paucity of rigorous theory and available data could make projections derived from simulation meaningless or, much worse, completely misleading. This objection would seem especially applicable for models of the entire human world, like Forrester's world dynamics model. (See in this regard Boulding [1973]). As Nardi notes, conditions most conducive to simulation modeling would occur in a limited subject with a good deal of theory behind it, such as in demography, economic analysis, population genetics or the like.

In general, the treatment of simulation seemed very judicious, with one lapse which must be regarded. At one point Nardi claims that the study of sociocultural change is vital. She states that "it is only by virtue of an observable change in one parameter that we can isolate the relationships between various types of cultural phenomena by observing the changes produced in other areas. . . . Without change, an institution or belief (or whatever) remains an environmental constant, and its effects on other aspects of the sociocultural system will go undetected."

Without denying the importance of sociocultural change for theory development, there are some problems with this position. For one thing, oscillating or cyclical shifts can also provide the information specified, even if they are not truly sociocultural change as commonly conceived. For another thing, the statement represents a position of strong empiricism in saying that one can only *discover* relationships empirically. It is doubtless true that we can only *prove* relationships empirically, but it does not follow that theory must stem from such observation. The classical argument in the history of science between the Baconians and the Cartesians has considered this issue of the relative value of approaching theory through empirical observation or through deduction.

When making her prediction, Nardi notes that this is a hypothetical exercise designed to test whether hunting-gathering societies *could* survive (i.e., maintain adequate populations) under specified conditions. It seemed to me that the analysis here was precisely the sort of task for which simulation is well suited, and I should like to offer only one caveat.

Insofar as her analysis destroys the position of the "flux" school that hunting-gathering societies *could not* survive with strict lineage exogamy, all is well. So also is her conclusion that, *under the test assumptions,* population could be maintained for lineage exogomous societies only under polygyny. However there are times when she seems to draw conclusions about the practical importance of the model that obscure the existence of a necessary assumption that average family size would not change. But if decline in population became sufficiently marked to be noticeable over a generation or two[10] either the rules might change or the norm for family size could grow larger. This caveat does not criticize Nardi's model or findings but only points toward a slight tendency to inflate its importance in practical terms.

SOME GENERAL COMMENTS

I want to put forward a conception of a good prediction that will sound fairly positivistic. In fact, it is taken (with a bit of liberty) from Karl Popper, who maintained he was not a positivist but who was generally viewed as a member of this persuasion.

Part of the conception was included in the mandate for the symposium on which this volume is based: a good prediction must be vulnerable. It must be capable of disproof. I agree completely but must add some more criteria. A good prediction also "forbids certain things to happen" (Popper 1965: 35–37), and it should forbid what one would ordinarily *expect.* Popper gives the example of Einstein's prediction that light will bend near a huge mass (a star). This is an outstanding prediction because it is vulnerable, forbids certain outcomes, and indeed forbids outcomes we would otherwise expect.[11]

Why, it might be asked, should one insist upon surprise or the unexpected as a virtue of the best predictions? The reason is that otherwise we risk endorsing what C. Wright Mills (1959) called "bureaucratic prediction," for example, a prediction from a political scientist that there will be a federal election in the United States in 1980. Predictions can be extremely mundane and trivial, and we have to engage them on the elusive but vital dimension of importance. One way to do this is to value the characteristic of the surprise or the unexpected.

Having set forth these criteria, I would next like to evaluate the papers for this symposium in terms of their predictions. As was noted at the outset, the papers are of very high quality. Further, in terms of the two focuses of the symposium—sociocultural change and prediction—the papers also seemed, on the whole, to excel in their discussions of sociocultural change. They are all grounded in an expertise about their respective regions that I can only envy. The predictions on the whole, however, are disappointing. Some are tautological, or nearly so; some seem relatively immune to disproof (which is not a virtue); some are "bureaucratic predictions" in Mills's sense; some are mundane and ordinary—of the sort that a native to the region could easily make without resort to theory.

Probably this is to be expected in a pioneering effort of this sort, for neither anthropologists nor sociologists are accustomed to pursuing their ideas far enough to derive predictions from them. Perhaps that is sufficient for the present, for it seems that all participants have been "pushed" and stimulated by the symposium, myself included. The topic presented an unusual challenge; not all papers succeeded in meeting it. In some cases the predictions appeared as though they had been tacked on to what was essentially a very good paper on something else. But the fact that the challenge was unusual may have made it all the more fruitful. I am not entirely a positivist, but I feel that requiring prediction imposes a certain discipline on one's thinking—regardless of whether it is done for purposes of science or for applied interventionist reasons.

One of the papers cited the philosopher Harré to the effect that we should "do explanation and prediction will take care of itself." Great admirer of Harré that I am, this does not seem to me to be one of his brighter ideas. The proof of error is in our own entrails—sociology and anthropology themselves suffice to illustrate the folly of such a position. But further, I would propose turning the remark on its head: do prediction and theory will take care of itself. The reason for this is that prediction is the most demanding of the several tasks we encounter. It therefore imposes a degree of rigor on thinking and clears away a lot of nonsense. Quite apart from whether the social sciences can or should adopt a natural science model, they can and should attempt to predict in order to choose between competing theories and to distill the valuable parts of overextended theories.[12]

This is not to say that prediction should be the all-consuming interest. That would lead us to the premature rejection of good new theories or to disregard important explanations simply because they cannot predict —evolutionary theory in biology is a major illustration. The point is simply that anthropology and sociology are so far removed from this extreme that it poses no danger at present. The opposite danger, sloppy thinking unchecked by the demands of prediction, seems much more pressing.[13]

I suspect that a part of the neglect of prediction comes from the remoteness of sociology and anthropology from centers of power and practical importance. As is often noted, we are almost exclusively academic disciplines with few practitioners. There are no analogs to engineers or doctors pressing us for answers, and those persons in government who do have backgrounds in our disciplines seem to have found niches where they can explain events after the fact rather than being called upon to predict. I like to contrast our situation with that of the economists. They are indeed called upon to predict and often do quite poorly at it, but so far as I can see this obligation has led them to increase attention to certain subjects—e.g., simulation, leading indicators—that we in sociology and anthropology only come upon, if at all, when we chance to copy the economists.

To be sure there is the danger from excessive government involvement that one may be coopted and forced to live within the present system instead of speculating freely on alternative social arrangements. And indeed we can see this happening to some government economists. But I think, looking at the discipline of economics as a whole, this has not taken place. Rather, economics is in the position to offer blueprints of alternative economic arrangements with far greater confidence than we can offer alternatives, with specificity, in anthropology or sociology. I do not maintain that this ability is purely a result of economists' involvement in the government and prediction, since I do not believe this to be historically accurate. But it does seem to show that involvement of this kind does not preclude the consideration of alternative social structures. And it may facilitate it, indirectly, by increasing the discipline with which theories are conceived.

NOTES

1. No science is very good at prophecy, everyday conceptions of the natural sciences notwithstanding (see Henshel 1976, part 3).

2. To complete the connections, one wonders whether role incumbents might do their negotiating within the framework of an exchange perspective. We have a possible juncture here of role theory and exchange theory (see Thibaut and Kelley 1959). This is especially poignant where, at one point in the paper, it is maintained that roles change in response to social, economic, or political pressures—the state of affairs exchange theory is supposed to deal with (see Blau 1964). Ordinarily, exchange theory is employed to explain interpersonal behavior, but some of the literature (e.g., Homans 1961) suggests it might be applied to explain shifts in modal role activities by considering simultaneous pressures being exerted on a large number of role occupants.

3. The predictions about the future of specific roles, for instance, are ultimately entirely dependent on the acuity of the naming or labeling of the underlying role dimensions.

4. Parenthetically, the title of the paper mentions "extermination," a topic not covered except possibly in an extremely metaphorical sense.

5. One may be permitted to wonder what would happen if the emphasis on salvation in the religious teachings were replaced with an emphasis on the social gospel, as it was to a large extent in North America in the early 1900s (Hopkins 1967). If we accept the importance of the symbolic form of millenarianism and Pessar's linking of millenarianism with an emphasis on salvation, then a shift in religious teaching to the social gospel might simultaneously lead to a decline in millenarian movements and to a rise in politically oriented movements among religious adherents—possibly akin to the social democratic parties that formed elsewhere. Pessar's footnotes 11 and 13 encourage this speculation.

6. This new debate is not to be confused with the labeling of *individuals* as problem cases, a matter for different debate entirely. Pessar's point has been emphasized by theorists as divergent as Marx and Mosca.

7. See in Simmel the section entitled "The Behavior of the Centralized Group in Conflict." In Dahrendorf the relevant section is entitled "The Institutionalization of Class Conflict."

8. It is suggested in the paper that segmentary, polycentric, networked systems may become the dominant social organization of the future. If this were so, it might be a move toward a participatory democracy as analyzed by Benello and Roussopoulos (1971). I am more skeptical, however, for I see this development as primarily a phenomenon of the middle class of the United States, not pervasive throughout all classes and educational levels. (Of course, it is true that most social movements start out as middle class.) SPIN is a process of the well-off, the reasonably well educated, and it requires a degree of self-imposed restraint that makes it highly unlikely to become a technique utilized by a cross-section of the country. (See also Morrison [1973] in this connection.)

9. See on this point Leslie Wilkins (1965).

10. There could be several indicators of population decline in nonliterate societies—such as conspicuous vacancies in traditional roles.

11. Einstein also predicted how much the light would be bent. I am not sure that social prediction will ever attain such precision, and I think we should be content with directional predictions that meet the criteria.

12. The clearest statement I have seen on these particular virtues of prediction is to be found at several points in Gibbs (1972).

13. Here is a brief list, in alphabetical order, of works I highly recommend to those interested in working in social prediction. The listings (not necessarily the most recent works) are designed to give an overview of the various ways of approaching social prediction: Bauer (1966); Bell and Mau (1971); Cole (1973); Duncan (1969); Henshel (1976, 1978); Martino (1972); Maruyama (1963); and Polak (1952; 1973 in translation).

REFERENCES

Bauer, Raymond A., ed., 1966. *Social Indicators* (Cambridge, Mass.: MIT Press).

Bell, Wendell, and James A. Mau, eds., 1971. *The Sociology of the Future* (New York: Russell Sage).

Benello, C. George, and Dimitrios Roussopoulos, eds., 1971. *The Case for Participatory Democracy* (New York: Viking Press).

Blau, Peter, 1964. *Exchange and Power in Social Life* (New York: Wiley).

Blumer, Herbert, 1971. Social Problems as Collective Behavior. *Social Problems* 18: 298–306.

Boulding, Kenneth E., 1973. Zoom, Gloom, Doom and Room. *The New Republic* 11 August, pp. 25–27.

Cole, H. S. D., et al., 1973. *Models of Doom: A Critique of the Limits to Growth* (New York: Universe Books).

Dahrendorf, Ralf, 1959. *Class and Class Conflict in Industrial Society* (Stanford, Calif.: Stanford University Press).

Duncan, Otis Dudley, 1969. Social Forecasting: The State of the Art. *The Public Interest* 17: 102–38.

Gibbs, Jack P., 1972. *Sociological Theory Construction* (Hinsdale, Ill.: Dryden Press).

Hawkins, Richard, and Gary Tiedeman, 1975. *The Creation of Deviance* (Columbus, Ohio: Charles Merrill).

Henshel, Richard L., 1971. Sociology and Prediction. *The American Sociologist* 6: 213–20.

———, 1975a. Effects of Disciplinary Prestige on Predictive Accuracy: Distortions from Feedback Loops. *Futures* 7:92–106.

———, 1975b. Scientific Status and Boundaries of the Self-Fulfilling Prophecy. Paper presented to the annual meetings of the American Sociological Association. San Francisco, August 1975.

———, 1976. *On the Future of Social Prediction* (Indianapolis: Bobbs-Merrill).

———, 1978. Self-Altering Predictions. In *Handbook of Futures Research,* J. O. Fowles, ed. (Westport, Conn.: Greenwood Press, pp. 99–123).

Henshel, Richard L., and Leslie W. Kennedy, 1973. Self-Altering Prophecies: Consequences for the Feasibility of Social Prediction. *General Systems* 18: 119–26.

Homans, George C., 1961. *Social Behavior: Its Elementary Forms* (New York: Harcourt).

Hopkins, C. H., 1967. *The Rise of the Social Gospel in American Protestantism, 1865–1915* (New Haven, Conn.: Yale University Press).

Klapper, Joseph T., 1960. *The Effects of Mass Communication* (New York: Free Press).

Manis, Jerome G., 1976. *Analyzing Social Problems* (New York: Praeger).

Martino, Joseph P., ed., 1972. *An Introduction to Technical Forecasting* (London: Gordon and Beach).

Maruyama, Margorah, 1963. The Second Cybernetics: Deviation Amplifying Mutual Causal Processes. *American Scientist* 51: 164–79.

Mills, C. Wright, 1959. *The Sociological Imagination* (New York: Oxford).

Morrison, Denton E., 1973. The Environmental Movement: Conflict Dynamics. *Journal of Voluntary Action Research* 2: 74–85.

Polak, Fred, 1973 (1952). *The Image of the Future*, trans. Elise Boulding (New York: Elsevier).

Popper, Karl R., 1965. *Conjectures and Refutations*, 2nd ed., (New York: Basic Books).

Raser, John R., 1969. *Simulation and Society* (Boston: Allyn and Bacon).

Schuessler, Karl, 1968. Prediction. In *International Encyclopedia of the Social Sciences*, Vol. 12 (New York: Macmillan), pp. 418–25.

Simmel, Georg, 1955 (1923). *Conflict*, trans. Kurt H. Wolff (New York: Free Press of Glencoe).

Smelser, Neil J., 1963. *Theory of Collective Behavior* (New York: Free Press of Glencoe).

Tallman, Irving, 1976. *Passion, Action, and Politics: A Perspective on Social Problems and Social-Problem Solving* (San Francisco: Freeman).

Thibaut, John W., and Harold H. Kelley, 1959. *The Social Psychology of Groups* (New York: John Wiley).

Wilkins, Leslie T., 1965. *Social Deviance: Social Policy, Action and Research* (Englewood Cliffs, N.J.: Prentice-Hall).

The Case for Strong Basic Anthropology: Comments on the Problem of Prediction

FRED L. STRODTBECK

Herbert Simon has called our attention to the fact that sequences can be made meaningless in two ways. They can be chopped too finely, or they can be extended over such a long interval of time that they obscure process. The emphasis on prediction as the demanding, final criterion for the evaluation of scientific effort must be fitted within these constraints.

It seems attractive to take the general stance that at the boundary between science and practical affairs it is legitimate to place a high priority on advance description of the effects of programs. At the same time, the development of science requires backing and filling, engagement in concerns that are calculatedly unpractical and in digressions for esthetic closure. Scientists are exposed to adventitious data through their work on journals, and their sense of the problem is sharpened through discussions at scientific meetings. It is in this latter sense that the contributions in this volume have a function beyond the substantive knowledge they communicate: they relate to the process through which science is institutionalized. They are part of an internal dialogue in the discipline about the stance applied anthropology will take in response to the external pressure to predict. It is a dilemma that arises from knowing that as good as we are, we are not soothsayers. It is my guess that this institutional phrasing of questions about prediction will create context for my evaluation of the papers that will contrast with the perspective of my co-discussant, author of the very helpful work *On the Future of Social Predictions*.

To begin, let me essentially invert the order in which the papers appear in this volume in order to comment first on Adams's chapter on the Navajo. He expands the construct "prediction" in a way that reminds one of Polanyi's "personal constructs" in his explanation of why it is difficult to make predictions about the Navajo. He reminds us that we should look at the social organization surrounding the Indians' reservations. He suggests that it is not internal cohesiveness so much as it is external barriers to social exchange that create the social enclaves. While some anthropologists would like to proceed by working with classic structural truths, Adams eclectically looks at contemporary realities. He describes the public welfare syndrome, for instance. By giving support to Navajo who can't find work within a reasonable distance from the reservation, the federal government promotes more intensive use of land and smaller tracts for an increasing population. The net effect of public welfare on the Navajo is to promote the decline of sheep raising, which Adams believes is at the core of the collective values of the Navajo family.

Adams makes us understand that despite our wish to believe that configuration in cultural values sometimes resists shifts in cultural content, it is not probable that this axiom will hold true for the Navajo. The United States can compel the assimilation of the Navajo by breaking up the reservation. The United States can delay—perhaps even forestall—assimilation by preserving the reservation intact. The study of internal tribal process with the beguiling assumption of "other things equal" could easily carry applied anthropology away from the truths about power that Adams would pragmatically stress. It is sobering to realize that outcomes one might wish to predict are in the hands of units that are not only reading the predictions but are also revising their policies. The net effect of Adams's essay is to reduce concern about a simple outcome. This leaves readers with a heightened human interest in a process that they now can see in a deeper and more complex way.

The Nardi paper puts the game of prediction on its head. By formal modeling, she shows that if rules relating to lineage exogamy were applied without polygyny, then populations of hunting-gathering bands would decline. Since, historically, the bands persisted, new credence is given those theorists who feel that more flexible rules characterize band competition. Even the addition of a rule of limited polygyny prevents population decline. In short, by being candid about the fact that formal models map only the surface of the complexity of a society, an ethnographer can undertake a limited dialogue with a computer. There are some things the ethnographers can suppose to be true that the computer can identify as being unprovable or impossible. By going back to Nardi's model, instances of extramarital reproduction, adoption, exchange of personnel between lineages, and rule breaking can be evaluated for their effects. The way the formalism can be made to interact with the ethnography makes clear that a new tool of great importance is being evolved. It is not possible to give full assurance that the formalisms will not eventually have a sinister role in policy, but so long as the formalism game is played by anthropologists who know the literature, the auditing of that which we believe we know by this process can be of great importance.

Harding and Clement introduce a microcultural cognitive perspective. Even without reference to the volume's emphasis on the prediction of change, the use of role terms and activity concepts to put Ixil and Ladino response in the same analytical space is an accomplishment in itself. This was done in two steps. Respondents first answered the questions, "What types of people are there? What kinds of things does each given person do?" These materials were used to produce a frame with fifty roles tabulated against forty-eight activities. The respondent's task was simply to answer yes or no to whether an incumbent in the role would carry out the activity. The answers were recorded in the appropriate row and column. The subsequent multivariate manipulation is to locate, on a minimum number of dimensions, the roles in such a way that their distance from one another is roughly inversely proportional to their similarity. From inspection of the outcome, names can be given the dimensions on which the roles are located. For the Ixil, the dimensions are wealth, ceremonial stature, and alien as opposed to local identity. For Ladinos, the dimensions are moral-immoral, manual or nonmanual work, and alien or local identity. Ixil see their diviners as poor, ceremonial, and local, while Ladinos see Ixil diviners as moderately moral, manual (laborer), and local. It would have been interesting to read more similar results and be led to form personal constructs that used the structure of these results.

With regard to the prediction of change, the major premise of Harding and Clement is that there is more consensus about social roles than there is about the activities associated with them. This provides a stability of expectations while social change takes place in the process of negotiating the content of roles. This is an important operationalization of the symbolic interactionalist's perspective on social process. Not resting on these laurels, they tighten the logic of their inquiry again by introducing a hypothetical role of agricultural demonstrator (an extension worker). The authors describe how Ixil, in contrast with Ladinos, would respond if such a role were introduced. They have similar interpretations for the diviner. In short, the authors demonstrate a technique through which a very large number of innocuous responses are compressed into a bicultural structure that in turn can be drawn on for relatively short-run predictions. They do not err in a belief that cognitive structures predominate over other facets of social organization; they simply suggest that elicited responses index a biased spectrum of social realities that are present in the society and can be drawn on for purposes as diverse as theory building and applied interventions. The paper is hard to read even when one is familiar with prior similar studies, but like the Nardi paper, it expands our understanding of what prediction may mean, and it is worth the effort it demands.

Gerlach's "report from the front" is a bold comment on the energy war. If the author had been testing his ideas against the sociology devoted to influence networks (Ed Laumann's work, for example [Laumann and Pappi 1976]) or the writings of Simmel (1955) or Coleman (1957) on community conflict, the tenor of the paper would have invited academic quibbling. As it stands, the assertion that social organization in the future will be very segmenting, polycentric and similar to social movements goes audaciously in the face of those who tell us that big corporations are organized to protect their core technology. When a threat occurs, the response will be a highly centralized mobilization of resources. Since the "power grid" triumphed over the opponents to the power line in Gerlach's example, I read the paper as one in which the author argues against himself in a most disarming way.

In each of the final three papers to be discussed, the authors make their blending of method and substantive content smoothly—so smoothly that a commentator's task is to uncover the stubborn discipline that has given their final products the appearance of effortlessness. At the surface, Gallaher's restudy of family role relations in Ireland is very convincing. While telling us of a developing insistence on expressive gratification by Irish women, the author plants in our mind a new historical hypothesis. The reader begins to wonder if before the size of Irish farms declined, the expressive gratification of women was greater. A facet that was once a static element in a complex situation takes on new life as a dependent variable. The author leads the reader to speculate whether the low expressive gratification of women persisted so long because migration removed the segments of the population who would have changed institutions. We start to ask just what institutions (other than bars) are destined to change if the current trends are continued. Gallaher is a very good teacher because he gives you the latitude to participate in the explanation. A description of change that is three generations in depth must first stand up as substantive ethnography. Secondly, it must stimulate a retroductive process. A reader asks, in essence, "If these new trends are present, then what is the process that brought them about?" Finally, it should help the reader identify a more general perspective. In this latter connection, Gallaher seems to suggest that there was an interaction between sexual Puritanism and economic pressures that made those already deprived in their expressiveness even more demanding in their expectations for the behavior of others. If such a dynamic process was involved, Gallaher's more detailed description in later publications will be most welcome, for this may be a process of great importance in the prediction of shift in cultural emphases.

Social scientists frequently are tormented by the question of whether they confront an analysis of a continuing process or of a transformation of a system. Pessar's superbly erudite, historical analysis goes right to the heart of this distinction. Greater rationality of institutions grows out of earlier acts of distortion, inversion, and rejection. The author's analysis leaves one intriguing question: for false consciousness to arise, is it required that there be an immature state? If the author's answer is yes, then a bold new doctrine will have been stated.

Finally, the Daniels paper is helpfully nonlinear in its prediction that fuel pressures will restore a degree of pastoralization that will in turn help preserve an endangered culture. The Daniel paper reopens Adams's concern with the conditions of functional integrity in the face of great differences in relative power. The wide substantive and topical differences in the perspective on change that the three final papers represent remind us of the size of the task before us. A great deal of conventional anthropology will undoubtedly have to be completed before the potential of formal models of the type identified in Bonnie Nardi's paper can be utilized. In short, even though maintaining a low profile despite external pressure to predict social change may well be an exacting test of applied anthropology's professional maturity, it is reassuring to appreciate how clearly good applied work rests on the foundations of strong basic anthropology.

REFERENCES

Coleman, James S., 1957. *Community Conflict* (Glencoe, Ill.: Free Press).

Laumann, Edward O., and Franz U. Pappi, 1976. *Networks of Collective Action: A Perspective on Community Influence Systems* (New York: Academic Press).

Simmel, Georg, 1955. *Conflict,* trans. Kurt H. Wolff (Glencoe, Ill.: Free Press).

Simon, Herbert A., 1957. *Models of Man* (New York: John Wiley).

The Contributors

SUSAN ABBOTT is Assistant Professor of Anthropology and Behavioral Science at the University of Kentucky, Lexington. Her major research interests are medical anthropology with particular emphasis on the epidemiology of depression, comparative socialization, and social anthropology. Past research includes studies of rural Kenyan Kikuyu women's adaptations to macro economic and social change, the relations between ego development and social structure in a municipal bureaucracy in the midwestern United States, and value orientations and stress among adolescent Shoshoni, blacks, and whites in an Idaho Upward Bound Project for disadvantaged youth. Currently Abbott is analyzing data on the patterning of depressive symptomatology among Kikuyu while she is on leave to do two years of postdoctoral work in quantitative methods in the Department of Statistics at the University of California, Berkeley.

WILLIAM Y. ADAMS is Professor of Anthropology at the University of Kentucky, Lexington. He did early ethnological fieldwork among the Navajo and Hopi Indians but for the last twenty years has been primarily engaged in studies of the archaeology and culture history of Nubia and the Sudan. In the recent past Adams returned to the Navajo to do a followup study in the community where he first worked over twenty years ago.

DOROTHY C. CLEMENT is Associate Professor of Anthropology at the University of North Carolina, Chapel Hill. Her fields of interest are anthropology and education and language and culture, with emphasis on cognitive anthropology. She has conducted fieldwork in Trinidad, Guatemala, American Samoa, and the United States. Having recently finished a two-and-a-half-year ethnographic study, supported by the National Institute of Education, of an urban desegregated school, she is continuing to develop theoretical aspects of this investigation. Clement is particularly interested in the processes of generation and transmission of culture as knowledge systems and in the relationship of these processes to structural features of society.

ROBERT E. DANIELS is Assistant Professor of Anthropology at the University of North Carolina, Chapel Hill. During 1971–72 he was Field Director for the Child Development Research Unit, University of Nairobi, Kenya. His fieldwork has been concentrated in Kenya among the Kipsigis, but he has also done research among the Oglala Sioux. His major theoretical and substantive interests include psychological anthropology, systems theory, and African ethnology.

ART GALLAHER, JR., is Professor of Anthropology at the University of Kentucky, Lexington, where he also serves as Dean of the College of Arts and Sciences. His fields of interest are applied anthropology, culture change, intervention models, community study, and complex organizations. In addition to extensive fieldwork in Ireland, he has done research in the United States in the Ozarks, among Seminole Freedmen, and among blacks in Houston, Texas.

LUTHER P. GERLACH is Professor of Anthropology at the University of Minnesota. His research interests are in economic anthropology, sociocultural change, anthropology of social and religious movements, and human ecology. He has done fieldwork in East Africa, the Caribbean, Japan, Central America, Europe, and the United States. Gerlach has served as a member of the Energy Resources Lecture Team sponsored by the U.S. Information Agency, has been a participant in the "Societal Impact of Changing Images of Man" project of the Charles F. Kettering Foundation and Stanford Research Institute Team, and has served as a member of the Steering Committee of Future Choices: Energy Project of the Upper Midwest Council, as chairman of their Public Response Task Force and as a member of their Coal Advisory Board. He is now a member of their Environmental Mediation Task Force.

JOE R. HARDING is a project director with the Southern Regional Education Board in Atlanta, Georgia. He is also Research Assistant Professor in the Department of Anthropology, University of North Carolina, Chapel Hill, and president of the Policy Research and Planning Group, a nonprofit anthropological research organization. He has made use of the techniques of cognitive anthropology in a variety of research settings emphasizing the determination of acceptability and appropriateness of services and programs for particular cultural contexts. These have included Samoa, Korea, Nigeria, and a number of locations in the United States as well as in Guatemala, which is the setting for the work reported here. Currently he is directing a research and action project on the distribution of mental health professionals in the fourteen states of the South which make up the SREB region.

RICHARD L. HENSHEL is Associate Professor of Sociology at the University of Western Ontario. He has published a number of articles in sociology in the areas of deviance and social problems theory. He has authored a text on social problems policy and coedited a collection entitled *Perception in Criminology*. His other major interest is social prediction and self-fulfilling prophecy, which has led to his treatise *On the Future of Social Prediction*.

BONNIE A. NARDI is Visiting Lecturer in Anthropology at the University of North Carolina, Chapel Hill. Her research interests include population studies, gender roles, and economic anthropology, and her area of ethnographic interest is Oceania.

PATRICIA PESSAR is Assistant Professor of Anthropology at Duke University. Her research interests include symbolic anthropology, political anthropology, and social and cultural change. Pessar has done research in the Hebrides Islands of Scotland, in Black Tickle, Labrador, and in Santa Brigida, Bahia, Brazil.

FRED L. STRODTBECK is Professor of Sociology and Social Psychology at the University of Chicago. His past research has been concerned with small group process and with the relationship of values to social structure and process. This work has involved crosscultural research among the Navajo, Mormons, and Texan homesteaders in the American Southwest, Jewish and Italian families in the northeastern United States, and Mayan Indians in Yucatan, Mexico, where he directed a field research station. His current research is concerned with ego development in crosscultural settings and with the effects of quality of one's work life in the maintenance of differentiated personality.

JOHN VAN WILLIGEN is Associate Professor of Anthropology at the University of Kentucky, Lexington. He has studied community development among Papago Indians and has done manpower research for the Gila River Indian community, crosscultural management research in a Japanese-owned factory in rural Wisconsin, and research on the role of the reference librarian in the modern university. His current activities include research on the social dynamics of aging in a rural Kentucky community.